One Hundred Love Sonnets / *Cien sonetos de amor*

The Texas Pan American Series

Pablo Neruda and Matilde Urrutia

100 LOVE SONNETS

Cien sonetos de amor

BY PABLO NERUDA

Translated by Stephen Tapscott

University of Texas Press ◆ Austin

Fifteenth printing, 2002

Originally published as *Cien sonetos de amor*
© Editorial Losada, S. A., Buenos Aires, 1960

Requests for permission to reproduce material from this work
should be sent to Permissions, University of Texas Press,
Box 7819, Austin, Texas 78713-7819

∞ The paper used in this publication meets the minimum
requirements of American National Standard for Information
Sciences—Permanence of Paper for Printed Library Materials,
ANSI Z39.48-1984.

Library of Congress Cataloging-in-Publication Data
Neruda, Pablo, 1904–1973.
  One hundred love sonnets = Cien sonetos de amor.
  (Texas Pan American series)
  Includes index.
  1. Love poetry, Chilean—Translations into English. 2. Love
Poetry, English—Translations from Spanish. 3. Sonnets,
Chilean—Translations into English. 4. Sonnets, English—
Translations from Spanish. 5. Love poetry, Chilean. 6. Sonnets,
Chilean. I. Tapscott, Stephen, 1948– . II. Title. III. Title: Cien
sonetos de amor. IV. Series.
PQ8097.N4C513   1986   861   85-26421
ISBN 0-292-76028-0 (pbk.)

CONTENTS

TRANSLATOR'S NOTE

For some time now I have wanted to translate Pablo Neruda's *Cien sonetos de amor*, which first appeared in Spanish in 1960 but which is still virtually unknown to English-language readers. I was interested in working on these poems for several reasons. First, and above all, they are lovely work in the original Spanish: earthy, devout, political, adult. They are interesting for many reasons, historical and emotional and formal—including their nature as experiment: they represent Neruda's attempt to incorporate this affectionate, earthy, daily surrealist-and-political vision in a "classical" body, that of the sonnet.

My second reason for wanting to attempt a translation of these poems had to do with the received tradition of English-language poetry—and with a peculiarity of our culture. We don't have much of a tradition of love poetry in North America, and these poems seem to introduce attitudes of sensual joy of a sort that we—Anglophones, at least—have never been very comfortable with, nor very adept at expressing. Neruda seemed a natural choice, both because of his poems' own worth and because of what he might contribute to our North American tradition, a voice of intelligent sensual joy.

And, finally, I wanted to work on Neruda in general because our received sense of the shape of his career has been somewhat oddly determined by our own historical circumstances. We in the United States discovered Neruda during a period of our own turmoil in the 1960s; we seemed to need a poet who could be simultaneously affirmative, political, and emotionally generous, and we found him. In so doing, we tended to translate primarily the political Neruda (while avoiding for the most part his extremely Communist, even Stalinist, works) and, subsequently, the lovely early surrealist poems. Neruda's early *20 Love Poems and a Song of Despair* and the later *One Hundred Love Sonnets* are on the whole his most popular works in South America; once we can realign our concept of him a little, to see him first as a lyrical love poet working from that base, we can know him more fully and consistently. His more generous political spirit, his Allendist socialism, and his exuberance for physical realities and for a populist aesthetic all come from the same joyous Whitmanian impulses.

My first reasons for wanting to try a translation of the *Cien sonetos*, then, were to make some of the pleasure of Neruda's work available to English-speaking North Americans, to enlarge our own tradition slightly, and in part to correct our judgment of Neruda. I wanted to work on these poems in particular because I believed that something essential in them is in fact "translatable." Neruda calls these fourteen-line poems "sonnets," although he uses the traditional sonnet form in widely different ways—from a virtual free-verse order within the skeleton of a sonnet to rarer, more conventionally strict forms. Neruda clearly knows the Spanish traditions of the sonnet and the lyric-sequence; indeed, in these poems he sometimes plays against those conventions, as when he reverses the erotic/spiritual "Song of Songs" metaphors of San Juan de la Cruz and Santa Teresa, or when he uses the dynamic of the sequence to enlarge and to ramify continuous arguments. Neruda's own love sonnets most clearly exploit those conventions when he uses the traditional sonnet's ability to "turn" its argument, often by playing on the pivot between the octet and the sextet. His use of that conventional rhetorical structure of the sonnet is what most closely allies his own "sonnets" with the tradition. Neruda's particular innovation is his use of *voice*, in sound and in syntax, as the force that binds lines and stanzas into integrated wholes. That delicate adhesive force of the voice, that sense of organic information, like the sound of wood, is what an English version of these poems risks losing; not as much would be lost in terms of traditional "form" as might appear at first glance. And yet, in some essential way, I think, that sense of voice-as-formal-determinator is what is poetically "translatable" in these poems. At least, I hope so.

I subscribe to the principle that the fewer overt interpolations by the translator of a beautiful poem, the better. However, several other writers and critics and friends have helped me in this ambition to become as invisible as I can; their help, at least, should be acknowledged. For general information and orientation, I have relied heavily on Neruda's various memoirs, especially *Confieso que he vivido: Memorias*, edited by Matilde Neruda and Miguel Otero Silva, and also on the patient efficiency of David Ferriero and his staff in the Reference Department of the M.I.T. Humanities Library. For verbal models, I am grateful to earlier translators of Neruda's poems, including especially W. S. Merwin and Nathaniel Tarn. I have admired the luminous intuitions of Robert Bly and James Wright, in their early translations, and also the intelligence and respect-for-the-text of John Felstiner, in his book *Translating Neruda*. In Buenos Aires, Michael Falkner explained some of the rhythms by which Neruda carries his arguments. In Santiago and in Boston, Isabel Bize, with patience and good humor, helped me through unfamiliar South American idioms. Several other people have been particularly helpful in returning me to Neruda's idiomatic clarity, and in trying to keep me from introducing my own solecisms where Neruda's difficulties are lucid: my thanks to Tony Oquendo, Roberto Colón, and Steven Cramer, and to the scrupulous readers—Professors Ronald Christ and Gene Bell-Villada— and the staff at the University of Texas Press. I would like also to thank the Poetry Center of the 92nd Street YMHA, and the Rockefeller Foundation, for sponsoring me as a scholar-in-residence, with time and space to finish work on this project.

Finally: Neruda dedicated these poems to Matilde Urrutia. In modesty, I would like also to dedicate these translations to several sets of friends, to remember important occasions that punctuated my work on these poems: to Saul Touster and Irene Tayler, in honor of an important anniversary, and to Stephen Dobyns and Isabel Bize, as a belated wedding gift. And, of course, to the memory of Matilde Neruda.

SJT
Cambridge, Massachusetts

One Hundred Love Sonnets / *Cien sonetos de amor*

A MATILDE URRUTIA

Señora mía muy amada, gran padecimiento tuve al escribirte estos mal llamados sonetos y harto me dolieron y costaron, pero la alegría de ofrecértelos es mayor que una pradera. Al proponérmelo bien sabía que al costado de cada uno, por afición electiva y elegancia, los poetas de todo tiempo dispusieron rimas que sonaron como platería, cristal o cañonazo. Yo, con mucha humildad, hice estos sonetos de madera, les di el sonido de esta opaca y pura substancia y así deben llegar a tus oídos. Tú y yo caminando por bosques y arenales, por lagos perdidos, por cenicientas latitudes, recogimos fragmentos de palo puro, de maderos sometidos al vaivén del agua y la intemperie. De tales suavizadísimos vestigios construí con hacha, cuchillo, cortaplumas, *estas madererías de amor y edifiqué pequeñas casas de catorce tablas para que en ellas vivan tus ojos que adoro y canto. Así establecidas mis razones de amor te entrego esta centuria: sonetos de madera que sólo se levantaron porque tú les diste la vida.*

Octubre de 1959

TO MATILDE URRUTIA

My beloved wife, I suffered while I was writing these misnamed "sonnets"; they hurt me and caused me grief, but the happiness I feel in offering them to you is vast as a savanna. When I set this task for myself, I knew very well that down the right sides of sonnets, with elegant discriminating taste, poets of all times have arranged rhymes that sound like silver, or crystal, or cannonfire. But—with great humility—I made these sonnets out of wood; I gave them the sound of that opaque pure substance, and that is how they should reach your ears. Walking in forests or on beaches, along hidden lakes, in latitudes sprinkled with ashes, you and I have picked up pieces of pure bark, pieces of wood subject to the comings and goings of water and the weather. Out of such softened relics, then, with hatchet *and* machete *and* pocketknife, *I built up these lumber piles of love, and with fourteen boards each I built little houses, so that your eyes, which I adore and sing to, might live in them. Now that I have declared the foundations of my love, I surrender this century to you: wooden sonnets that rise only because you gave them life.*

October 1959

Morning / *Mañana*

*M*atilde, nombre de planta o piedra o vino,
de lo que nace de la tierra y dura,
palabra en cuyo crecimiento amanece,
en cuyo estío estalla la luz de los limones.

En ese nombre corren navíos de madera
rodeados por enjambres de fuego azul marino,
y esas letras son el agua de un río
que desemboca en mi corazón calcinado.

Oh nombre descubierto bajo una enredadera
como la puerta de un túnel desconocido
que comunica con la fragancia del mundo!

Oh invádeme con tu boca abrasadora,
indágame, si quieres, con tus ojos nocturnos,
pero en tu nombre déjame navegar y dormir.

Matilde: the name of a plant, or a rock, or a wine,
of things that begin in the earth, and last:
word in whose growth the dawn first opens,
in whose summer the light of the lemons bursts.

Wooden ships sail through that name,
and the fire-blue waves surround them:
its letters are the waters of a river
that pours through my parched heart.

O name that lies uncovered among tangling vines
like the door to a secret tunnel
toward the fragrance of the world!

Invade me with your hot mouth; interrogate me
with your night-eyes, if you want—only let me
steer like a ship through your name; let me rest there.

*A*mor, cuántos caminos hasta llegar a un beso,
qué soledad errante hasta tu compañía!
Siguen los trenes solos rodando con la lluvia.
En Taltal no amanece aún la primavera.

Pero tú y yo, amor mío, estamos juntos,
juntos desde la ropa a las raíces,
juntos de otoño, de agua, de caderas,
hasta ser sólo tú, sólo yo juntos.

Pensar que costó tantas piedras que lleva el río,
la desembocadura del agua de Boroa,
pensar que separados por trenes y naciones

tú y yo teníamos que simplemente amarnos,
con todos confundidos, con hombres y mujeres,
con la tierra que implanta y educa los claveles.

L ove, what a long way, to arrive at a kiss,
what loneliness-in-motion, toward your company!
Rolling with the rain we follow the tracks alone.
In Taltal there is neither daybreak nor spring.

But you and I, love, we are together
from our clothes down to our roots:
together in the autumn, in water, in hips, until
we can be alone together—only you, only me.

To think of the effort, that the current carried
so many stones, the delta of Boroa water;
to think that you and I, divided by trains and nations,

we had only to love one another:
with all the confusions, the men and the women,
the earth that makes carnations rise, and makes them bloom!

*Á*spero amor, violeta coronada de espinas,
matorral entre tantas pasiones erizado,
lanza de los dolores, corola de la cólera,
por qué caminos y cómo te dirigiste a mi alma?

Por qué precipitaste tu fuego doloroso,
de pronto, entre las hojas frías de mi camino?
Quién te enseñó los pasos que hasta mí te llevaron?
Qué flor, qué piedra, qué humo mostraron mi morada?

Lo cierto es que tembló la noche pavorosa,
el alba llenó todas las copas con su vino
y el sol estableció su presencia celeste,

mientras que el cruel amor me cercaba sin tregua
hasta que lacerándome con espadas y espinas
abrió en mi corazón un camino quemante.

B itter love, a violet with its crown
of thorns in a thicket of spiky passions,
spear of sorrow, corolla of rage: how did you come
to conquer my soul? What *via dolorosa* brought you?

Why did you pour your tender fire
so quickly, over my life's cool leaves?
Who pointed the way to you? What flower,
what rock, what smoke showed you where I live?

Because the earth shook—it did—, that awful night;
then dawn filled all the goblets with its wine;
the heavenly sun declared itself;

while inside, a ferocious love wound around
and around me—till it pierced me with its thorns, its sword,
slashing a seared road through my heart.

*R*ecordarás aquella quebrada caprichosa
a donde los aromas palpitantes treparon,
de cuando en cuando un pájaro vestido
con agua y lentitud: traje de invierno.

Recordarás los dones de la tierra:
irascible fragancia, barro de oro,
hierbas del matorral, locas raíces,
sortílegas espinas como espadas.

Recordarás el ramo que trajiste,
ramo de sombra y agua con silencio,
ramo como una piedra con espuma.

Y aquella vez fue como nunca y siempre:
vamos allí donde no espera nada
y hallamos todo lo que está esperando.

You will remember that leaping stream
where sweet aromas rose and trembled,
and sometimes a bird, wearing water
and slowness, its winter feathers.

You will remember those gifts from the earth:
indelible scents, gold clay,
weeds in the thicket and crazy roots,
magical thorns like swords.

You'll remember the bouquet you picked,
shadows and silent water,
bouquet like a foam-covered stone.

That time was like never, and like always.
So we go there, where nothing is waiting;
we find everything waiting there.

No te toque la noche ni el aire ni la aurora,
sólo la tierra, la virtud de los racimos,
las manzanas que crecen oyendo el agua pura,
el barro y las resinas de tu país fragante.

Desde Quinchamalí donde hicieron tus ojos
hasta tus pies creados para mí en la Frontera
eres la greda oscura que conozco:
en tus caderas toco de nuevo todo el trigo.

Tal vez tú no sabías, araucana,
que cuando antes de amarte me olvidé de tus besos
mi corazón quedó recordando tu boca

y fui como un herido por las calles
hasta que comprendí que había encontrado,
amor, mi territorio de besos y volcanes.

I did not hold your night, or your air, or the dawn:
only the earth, the truth of the fruit in clusters,
the apples that swell as they drink the sweet water,
the clay and the resins of your sweet-smelling land.

From Quinchamalí where your eyes began
to the Frontera where your feet were made for me,
you are my dark familiar clay:
holding your hips, I hold the wheat in its fields again.

Woman from Arauco, maybe you didn't know
how before I loved you I forgot your kisses.
But my heart went on, remembering your mouth—and I
    went on

and on through the streets like a man wounded,
until I understood, Love: I had found
my place, a land of kisses and volcanoes.

En los bosques, perdido, corté una rama oscura
y a los labios, sediento, levanté su susurro:
era tal vez la voz de la lluvia llorando,
una campana rota o un corazón cortado.

Algo que desde tan lejos me parecía
oculto gravemente, cubierto por la tierra,
un grito ensordecido por inmensos otoños,
por la entreabierta y húmeda tiniebla de las hojas.

Pero allí, despertando de los sueños del bosque,
la rama de avellano cantó bajo mi boca
y su errabundo olor trepó por mi criterio

como si me buscaran de pronto las raíces
que abandoné, la tierra perdida con mi infancia,
y me detuve herido por el aroma errante.

Lost in the forest, I broke off a dark twig
and lifted its whisper to my thirsty lips:
maybe it was the voice of the rain crying,
a cracked bell, or a torn heart.

Something from far off: it seemed
deep and secret to me, hidden by the earth,
a shout muffled by huge autumns,
by the moist half-open darkness of the leaves.

Wakening from the dreaming forest there, the hazel-sprig
sang under my tongue, its drifting fragrance
climbed up through my conscious mind

as if suddenly the roots I had left behind
cried out to me, the land I had lost with my childhood—
and I stopped, wounded by the wandering scent.

"Vendrás conmigo" dije—sin que nadie supiera
dónde y cómo latía mi estado doloroso,
y para mí no había clavel ni barcarola,
nada sino una herida por el amor abierta.

Repetí: ven conmigo, como si me muriera,
y nadie vio en mi boca la luna que sangraba,
nadie vio aquella sangre que subía al silencio.
Oh amor ahora olvidemos la estrella con espinas!

Por eso cuando oí que tu voz repetía
"Vendrás conmigo"—fue como si desataras
dolor, amor, la furia del vino encarcelado

que desde su bodega sumergida subiera
y otra vez en mi boca sentí un sabor de llama,
de sangre y de claveles, de piedra y quemadura.

C*ome with me*, I said, and no one knew
where, or how my pain throbbed,
no carnations or barcaroles for me,
only a wound that love had opened.

I said it again: *Come with me*, as if I were dying,
and no one saw the moon that bled in my mouth
or the blood that rose into the silence.
O Love, now we can forget the star that has such thorns!

That is why, when I heard your voice repeat
Come with me, it was as if you had let loose
the grief, the love, the fury of a cork-trapped wine

that geysers flooding from deep in its vault:
in my mouth I felt the taste of fire again,
of blood and carnations, of rock and scald.

Si no fuera porque tus ojos tienen color de luna,
de día con arcilla, con trabajo, con fuego,
y aprisionada tienes la agilidad del aire,
si no fuera porque eres una semana de ámbar,

si no fuera porque eres el momento amarillo
en que el otoño sube por las enredaderas
y eres aún el pan que la luna fragante
elabora paseando su harina por el cielo,

oh, bienamada, yo no te amaría!
En tu abrazo yo abrazo lo que existe,
la arena, el tiempo, el árbol de la lluvia,

y todo vive para que yo viva:
sin ir tan lejos puedo verlo todo:
veo en tu vida todo lo viviente.

If your eyes were not the color of the moon,
of a day full of clay, and work, and fire,
if even held-in you did not move in agile grace like the air,
if you were not an amber week,

not the yellow moment
when autumn climbs up through the vines;
if you were not that bread the fragrant moon
kneads, sprinkling its flour across the sky,

oh, my dearest, I could not love you so!
But when I hold you I hold everything that is—
sand, time, the tree of the rain,

everything is alive so that I can be alive:
without moving I can see it all:
in your life I see everything that lives.

Al golpe de la ola contra la piedra indócil
la claridad estalla y establece su rosa
y el círculo del mar se reduce a un racimo,
a una sola gota de sal azul que cae.

Oh radiante magnolia desatada en la espuma,
magnética viajera cuya muerte florece
y eternamente vuelve a ser y a no ser nada:
sal rota, deslumbrante movimiento marino.

Juntos tú y yo, amor mío, sellamos el silencio,
mientras destruye el mar sus constantes estatuas
y derrumba sus torres de arrebato y blancura,

porque en la trama de estos tejidos invisibles
del agua desbocada, de la incesante arena,
sostenemos la única y acosada ternura.

*T*here where the waves shatter on the restless rocks
the clear light bursts and enacts its rose,
and the sea-circle shrinks to a cluster of buds,
to one drop of blue salt, falling.

O bright magnolia bursting in the foam,
magnetic transient whose death blooms
and vanishes—being, nothingness—forever:
broken salt, dazzling lurch of the sea.

You and I, Love, together we ratify the silence,
while the sea destroys its perpetual statues,
collapses its towers of wild speed and whiteness:

because in the weavings of those invisible fabrics,
galloping water, incessant sand,
we make the only permanent tenderness.

Suave es la bella como si música y madera,
ágata, telas, trigo, duraznos transparentes,
hubieran erigido la fugitiva estatua.
Hacia la ola dirige su contraria frescura.

El mar moja bruñidos pies copiados
a la forma recién trabajada en la arena
y es ahora su fuego femenino de rosa
una sola burbuja que el sol y el mar combaten.

Ay, que nada te toque sino la sal del frío!
Que ni el amor destruya la primavera intacta.
Hermosa, reverbero de la indeleble espuma,

deja que tus caderas impongan en el agua
una medida nueva de cisne o de nenúfar
y navegue tu estatua por el cristal eterno.

This beauty is soft—as if music and wood,
agate, cloth, wheat, peaches the light shines through
had made an ephemeral statue.
And now she sends her freshness out, against the waves.

The sea dabbles at those tanned feet, repeating
their shape, just imprinted in the sand.
And now she is the womanly fire of a rose,
the only bubble the sun and the sea contend against.

Oh, may nothing touch you but the chilly salt!
May not even love disturb that unbroken springtime!
Beautiful woman, echo of the endless foam,

may your statuesque hips in the water make
a new measure—a swan, a lily—, as you float
your form through that eternal crystal.

*T*engo hambre de tu boca, de tu voz, de tu pelo
y por las calles voy sin nutrirme, callado,
no me sostiene el pan, el alba me desquicia,
busco el sonido líquido de tus pies en el día.

Estoy hambriento de tu risa resbalada,
de tus manos color de furioso granero,
tengo hambre de la pálida piedra de tus uñas,
quiero comer tu piel como una intacta almendra.

Quiero comer el rayo quemado en tu hermosura,
la nariz soberana del arrogante rostro,
quiero comer la sombra fugaz de tus pestañas

y hambriento vengo y voy olfateando el crepúsculo
buscándote, buscando tu corazón caliente
como un puma en la soledad de Quitratúe.

I crave your mouth, your voice, your hair.
Silent and starving, I prowl through the streets.
Bread does not nourish me, dawn disrupts me, all day
I hunt for the liquid measure of your steps.

I hunger for your sleek laugh,
your hands the color of a savage harvest,
hunger for the pale stones of your fingernails,
I want to eat your skin like a whole almond.

I want to eat the sunbeam flaring in your lovely body,
the sovereign nose of your arrogant face,
I want to eat the fleeting shade of your lashes,

and I pace around hungry, sniffing the twilight,
hunting for you, for your hot heart,
like a puma in the barrens of Quitratúe.

Plena mujer, manzana carnal, luna caliente,
espeso aroma de algas, lodo y luz machacados,
qué oscura claridad se abre entre tus columnas?
Qué antigua noche el hombre toca con sus sentidos?

Ay, amar es un viaje con agua y con estrellas,
con aire ahogado y bruscas tempestades de harina:
amar es un combate de relámpagos
y dos cuerpos por una sola miel derrotados.

Beso a beso recorro tu pequeño infinito,
tus márgenes, tus ríos, tus pueblos diminutos,
y el fuego genital transformado en delicia

corre por los delgados caminos de la sangre
hasta precipitarse como un clavel nocturno,
hasta ser y no ser sino un rayo en la sombra.

Full woman, flesh-apple, hot moon,
thick smell of seaweed, mud and light in masquerade,
what secret clarity opens through your columns?
What ancient night does a man touch with his senses?

Oh, love is a journey with water and stars,
with drowning air and storms of flour;
love is a clash of lightnings,
two bodies subdued by one honey.

Kiss by kiss I travel your little infinity,
your borders, your rivers, your tiny villages;
and a genital fire—transformed, delicious—

slips through the narrow roadways of the blood
till it pours itself, quick, like a night carnation, till it is:
and is nothing, in shadow, and a flimmer of light.

*L*a luz que de tus pies sube a tu cabellera,
la turgencia que envuelve tu forma delicada,
no es de nácar marino, nunca de plata fría:
eres de pan, de pan amado por el fuego.

La harina levantó su granero contigo
y creció incrementada por la edad venturosa,
cuando los cereales duplicaron tu pecho
mi amor era el carbón trabajando en la tierra.

Oh, pan tu frente, pan tus piernas, pan tu boca,
pan que devoro y nace con luz cada mañana,
bienamada, bandera de las panaderías,

una lección de sangre te dio el fuego,
de la harina aprendiste a ser sagrada,
y del pan el idioma y el aroma.

The light that rises from your feet to your hair,
the strength enfolding your delicate form,
are not mother-of-pearl, not chilly silver:
you are made of bread, a bread the fire adores.

The grain grew high in its harvest, in you,
in good time the flour swelled;
as the dough rose, doubling your breasts,
my love was the coal waiting ready in the earth.

Oh, bread your forehead, your legs, your mouth,
bread I devour, born with the morning light,
my love, beacon-flag of the bakeries:

fire taught you a lesson of the blood;
you learned your holiness from flour,
from bread your language and aroma.

$\mathcal{M}$e falta tiempo para celebrar tus cabellos.
Uno por uno debo contarlos y alabarlos:
otros amantes quieren vivir con ciertos ojos,
yo sólo quiero ser tu peluquero.

En Italia te bautizaron Medusa
por la encrespada y alta luz de tu cabellera.
Yo te llamo chascona mía y enmarañada:
mi corazón conoce las puertas de tu pelo.

Cuando tú te extravíes en tus propios cabellos,
no me olvides, acuérdate que te amo,
no me dejes perdido ir sin tu cabellera

por el mundo sombrío de todos los caminos
que sólo tiene sombra, transitorios dolores,
hasta que el sol sube a la torre de tu pelo.

I don't have time enough to celebrate your hair.
One by one I should detail your hairs and praise them.
Other lovers want to live with particular eyes;
I only want to be your stylist.

In Italy they called you *Medusa*,
because of the high bristling light of your hair.
I call you *curly*, *my tangler*;
my heart knows the doorways of your hair.

When you lose your way through your own hair,
do not forget me, remember that I love you.
Don't let me wander lost—without your hair—

through the dark world, webbed by empty
roads with their shadows, their roving sorrows,
till the sun rises, lighting the high tower of your hair.

Desde hace mucho tiempo la tierra te conoce:
eres compacta como el pan o la madera,
eres cuerpo, racimo de segura substancia,
tienes peso de acacia, de legumbre dorada.

Sé que existes no sólo porque tus ojos vuelan
y dan luz a las cosas como ventana abierta,
sino porque de barro te hicieron y cocieron
en Chillán, en un horno de adobe estupefacto.

Los seres se derraman como aire o agua o frío
y vagos son, se borran al contacto del tiempo,
como si antes de muertos fueran desmenuzados.

Tú caerás conmigo como piedra en la tumba
y así por nuestro amor que no fue consumido
continuará viviendo con nosotros la tierra.

$\mathcal{T}$he earth has known you for a long time now:
you are as firm as bread, or wood;
you are a body, a cluster of absolute substances;
you have an acacia's gravity, the weight of a golden vegetable.

I know you exist, not only because your eyes fly open
and shed their light on things, like an open window—
but also because you were molded in clay, you were fired
in Chillán, in an astounded adobe oven.

Beings: they dissolve like the air, or water, or the cold.
And they are vague, they vanish when time touches them,
as if before death they crumbled into dust.

But you will fall with me like a rock into the grave:
thanks to our love, which will never waste away,
the earth will continue to live.

Amo el trozo de tierra que tú eres,
porque de las praderas planetarias
otra estrella no tengo. Tú repites
la multiplicación del universo.

Tus anchos ojos son la luz que tengo
de las constelaciones derrotadas,
tu piel palpita como los caminos
que recorre en la lluvia el meteoro.

De tanta luna fueron para mí tus caderas,
de todo el sol tu boca profunda y su delicia,
de tanta luz ardiente como miel en la sombra

tu corazón quemado por largos rayos rojos,
y así recorro el fuego de tu forma besándote,
pequeña y planetaria, paloma y geografía.

I love the handful of the earth you are.
Because of its meadows, vast as a planet,
I have no other star. You are my replica
of the multiplying universe.

Your wide eyes are the only light I know
from extinguished constellations;
your skin throbs like the streak
of a meteor through rain.

Your hips were that much of the moon for me;
your deep mouth and its delights, that much sun;
your heart, fiery with its long red rays,

was that much ardent light, like honey in the shade.
So I pass across your burning form, kissing
you—compact and planetary, my dove, my globe.

No te amo como si fueras rosa de sal, topacio
o flecha de claveles que propagan el fuego:
te amo como se aman ciertas cosas oscuras,
secretamente, entre la sombra y el alma.

Te amo como la planta que no florece y lleva
dentro de sí, escondida, la luz de aquellas flores,
y gracias a tu amor vive oscuro en mi cuerpo
el apretado aroma que ascendió de la tierra.

Te amo sin saber cómo, ni cuándo, ni de dónde,
te amo directamente sin problemas ni orgullo:
así te amo porque no sé amar de otra manera,

sino así de este modo en que no soy ni eres,
tan cerca que tu mano sobre mi pecho es mía,
tan cerca que se cierran tus ojos con mi sueño.

I do not love you as if you were salt-rose, or topaz,
or the arrow of carnations the fire shoots off.
I love you as certain dark things are to be loved,
in secret, between the shadow and the soul.

I love you as the plant that never blooms
but carries in itself the light of hidden flowers;
thanks to your love a certain solid fragrance,
risen from the earth, lives darkly in my body.

I love you without knowing how, or when, or from where.
I love you straightforwardly, without complexities or pride;
so I love you because I know no other way

than this: where *I* does not exist, nor *you*,
so close that your hand on my chest is my hand,
so close that your eyes close as I fall asleep.

Por las montañas vas como viene la brisa
o la corriente brusca que baja de la nieve
o bien tu cabellera palpitante confirma
los altos ornamentos del sol en la espesura.

Toda la luz del Cáucaso cae sobre tu cuerpo
como en una pequeña vasija interminable
en que el agua se cambia de vestido y de canto
a cada movimiento transparente del río.

Por los montes el viejo camino de guerreros
y abajo enfurecida brilla como una espada
el agua entre murallas de manos minerales,

hasta que tú recibes de los bosques de pronto
el ramo o el relámpago de unas flores azules
y la insólita flecha de un aroma salvaje.

*Y*ou move through the mountains like a breeze,
like a quick stream dropping from under the snow:
your hair in its thickness throbs like the high
adornments of the sun, repeating them for me.

All the light of the Caucasus falls across your body
like a little vase, infinitely refractive,
in which the water changes clothes and sings
with every motion of the distant river.

The old warrior road winds through the hills, and, below,
the old army fortifications: the water they hold
in their mineral hands shines fierce as a sword:

till the woods send toward you
suddenly a sprig—a lightning bolt—of a few blue flowers,
the strange-wild arrow of their forest smell.

Mientras la magna espuma de Isla Negra,
la sal azul, el sol en las olas te mojan,
yo miro los trabajos de la avispa
empeñada en la miel de su universo.

Va y viene equilibrando su recto y rubio vuelo
como si deslizara de un alambre invisible
la elegancia del baile, la sed de su cintura,
y los asesinatos del aguijón maligno.

De petróleo y naranja es su arco iris,
busca como un avión entre la hierba,
con un rumor de espiga vuela, desaparece,

mientras que tú sales del mar, desnuda,
y regresas al mundo llena de sal y sol,
reverberante estatua y espada de la arena.

*W*hile the huge seafoam of Isla Negra,
the blue salt, the sun in the waves splash over you,
I watch the bee at its work,
avid in the honey of its universe.

It comes and it leaves, balancing its straight pale flight
as if it slid on invisible wires:
its elegant dance, its thirsty waist,
the assassinations of its mean little needle.

Through an orange-and-gasoline rainbow
it hunts, like an airplane in the grasses;
it flies with a hint of a spike; it disappears;

while you come naked out of the sea
and return to the world full of salt and sun:
reverberating statue, sword in the sand.

Mi fea, eres una castaña despeinada,
mi bella, eres hermosa como el viento,
mi fea, de tu boca se pueden hacer dos,
mi bella, son tus besos frescos como sandías.

Mi fea, dónde están escondidos tus senos?
Son mínimos como dos copas de trigo.
Me gustaría verte dos lunas en el pecho:
las gigantescas torres de tu soberanía.

Mi fea, el mar no tiene tus uñas en su tienda,
mi bella, flor a flor, estrella por estrella,
ola por ola, amor, he contado tu cuerpo:

mi fea, te amo por tu cintura de oro,
mi bella, te amo por una arruga en tu frente,
amor, te amo por clara y por oscura.

*M*y ugly love, you're a messy chestnut.
My beauty, you are pretty as the wind.
Ugly: your mouth is big enough for two mouths.
Beauty: your kisses are fresh as new melons.

Ugly: where *did* you hide your breasts?
They're meager, two little scoops of wheat.
I'd much rather see two moons across your chest,
two huge proud towers.

Ugly: not even the sea contains things like your toenails.
Beauty: flower by flower, star by star, wave by wave,
Love, I've made an inventory of your body:

My ugly one, I love you for your waist of gold;
my beauty, for the wrinkle on your forehead.
My Love: I love you for your clarity, your dark.

*O*h que todo el amor propague en mí su boca,
que no sufra un momento más sin primavera,
yo no vendí sino mis manos al dolor,
ahora, bienamada, déjame con tus besos.

Cubre la luz del mes abierto con tu aroma,
cierra las puertas con tu cabellera,
y en cuanto a mí no olvides que si despierto y lloro
es porque en sueños sólo soy un niño perdido

que busca entre las hojas de la noche tus manos,
el contacto del trigo que tú me comunicas,
un rapto centelleante de sombra y energía.

Oh, bienamada, y nada más que sombra
por donde me acompañes en tus sueños
y me digas la hora de la luz.

If only love would spread its savor through me!
—not to go one moment more without spring!
What I sold into sorrow was only my hands,
dearest: now leave me with your kisses.

Shut out the month's light with your fragrance; .
close all the doors with your hair.
Only do not forget, if I wake up crying
it's only because in my dream I'm a lost child

hunting through the leaves of the night for your hands,
for your caresses like the wheat,
the flashing rapture of shadow and energy.

O my dearest, nothing but shadow there
where you walk with me through your dream:
you tell me when the light returns.

*C*uántas veces, amor, te amé sin verte y tal vez
   sin recuerdo,
sin reconocer tu mirada, sin mirarte, centaura,
en regiones contrarias, en un mediodía quemante:
eras sólo el aroma de los cereales que amo.

Tal vez te vi, te supuse al pasar levantando una copa
en Angol, a la luz de la luna de junio,
o eras tú la cintura de aquella guitarra
que toqué en las tinieblas y sonó como el mar desmedido.

Te amé sin que yo lo supiera, y busqué tu memoria.
En las casas vacías entré con linterna a robar tu retrato.
Pero yo ya sabía cómo eras. De pronto

mientras ibas conmigo te toqué y se detuvo mi vida:
frente a mis ojos estabas, reinándome, y reinas.
Como hoguera en los bosques el fuego es tu reino.

Love, how often I loved you without seeing—
without remembering you—
not recognizing your glance, not knowing you, a gentian
in the wrong place, scorching in the hot noon,
but I loved only the smell of the wheat.

Or maybe I saw you, imagined you lifting a wineglass
in Angol, by the light of the summer's moon;
or were you the waist of that guitar I strummed
in the shadows, the one that rang like an impetuous sea?

I loved you without knowing I did; I searched to remember you.
I broke into houses to steal your likeness,
though I already knew what you were like. And, suddenly,

when you were there with me I touched you, and my life
stopped: you stood before me, you took dominion like a queen:
like a wildfire in the forest, and the flame is your dominion.

*F*ue luz el fuego y pan la luna rencorosa,
el jazmín duplicó su estrellado secreto,
y del terrible amor las suaves manos puras
dieron paz a mis ojos y sol a mis sentidos.

Oh amor, cómo de pronto, de las desgarraduras
hiciste el edificio de la dulce firmeza,
derrotaste las uñas malignas y celosas
y hoy frente al mundo somos como una sola vida.

Así fue, así es y así será hasta cuando,
salvaje y dulce amor, bienamada Matilde,
el tiempo nos señale la flor final del día.

Sin ti, sin mí, sin luz ya no seremos:
entonces más allá de la tierra y la sombra
el resplandor de nuestro amor seguirá vivo.

The fire for light, a rancorous moon for bread,
the jasmine smearing around its bruised secrets:
then from a terrifying love, soft white hands
poured peace into my eyes and sun into my senses.

O love, how quickly you built a sweet
firmness where the wounds had been!
You fought off the talons and claws, and now
we stand as a single life before the world.

That's how it was, how it is, how it will be,
my wild sweet love, my dearest Matilde,
till time signals us with the day's last flower:

then there will be no you, no me, no light,
and yet beyond the earth, beyond its shadowy dark,
the splendor of our love will be alive.

*A*mor, amor, las nubes a la torre del cielo
subieron como triunfantes lavanderas,
y todo ardió en azul, todo fue estrella:
el mar, la nave, el día se desterraron juntos.

Ven a ver los cerezos del agua constelada
y la clave redonda del rápido universo,
ven a tocar el fuego del azul instantáneo,
ven antes de que sus pétalos se consuman.

No hay aquí sino luz, cantidades, racimos,
espacio abierto por las virtudes del viento
hasta entregar los últimos secretos de la espuma.

Y entre tantos azules celestes, sumergidos,
se pierden nuestros ojos adivinando apenas
los poderes del aire, las llaves submarinas.

Love, love, the clouds went up the tower of the sky
like triumphant washerwomen, and it all
glowed in blue, all like a single star,
the sea, the ship, the day were all exiled together.

Come see the cherries of the water in the weather,
the round key to the universe, which is so quick:
come touch the fire of this momentary blue,
before its petals wither.

There's nothing here but light, quantities, clusters,
space opened by the graces of the wind
till it gives up the final secret of the foam.

Among so many blues—heavenly blues, sunken blues—
our eyes are a little confused: they can hardly divine
the powers of the air, the keys to the secrets in the sea.

Antes de amarte, amor, nada era mío:
vacilé por las calles y las cosas:
nada contaba ni tenía nombre:
el mundo era del aire que esperaba.

Yo conocí salones cenicientos,
túneles habitados por la luna,
hangares crueles que se despedían,
preguntas que insistían en la arena.

Todo estaba vacío, muerto y mudo,
caído, abandonado y decaído,
todo era inalienablemente ajeno,

todo era de los otros y de nadie,
hasta que tu belleza y tu pobreza
llenaron el otoño de regalos.

Before I loved you, Love, nothing was my own:
I wavered through the streets, among objects:
nothing mattered or had a name:
the world was made of air, which waited.

I knew rooms full of ashes,
tunnels where the moon lived,
rough warehouses that growled *Get lost*,
questions that insisted in the sand.

Everything was empty, dead, mute,
fallen, abandoned, and decayed:
inconceivably alien, it all

belonged to someone else—to no one:
till your beauty and your poverty
filled the autumn plentiful with gifts.

Ni el color de las dunas terribles en Iquique,
ni el estuario del Río Dulce de Guatemala,
cambiaron tu perfil conquistado en el trigo,
tu estilo de uva grande, tu boca de guitarra.

Oh corazón, oh mía desde todo el silencio,
desde las cumbres donde reinó la enredadera
hasta las desoladas planicies del platino,
en toda patria pura te repitió la tierra.

Pero ni huraña mano de montes minerales,
ni nieve tibetaña, ni piedra de Polonia,
nada alteró tu forma de cereal viajero,

como si greda o trigo, guitarras o racimos
de Chillán defendieran en ti su territorio
imponiendo el mandato de la luna silvestre.

Neither the color of Iquique's awesome dunes,
nor the inlet of Guatemala's Río Dulce: nothing
has changed your profile, subdued in the wheat,
nor your plump-grape form, nor your guitar-mouth.

O my heart, my own, since before all silence,
from the uplands ruled by tangling vines
to the desolate platinum prairies: in every pure
landscape, the earth has imitated you.

But not even the shy mineral hands of the hills,
nor the snows of Tibet, nor the stones of Poland—nothing
has altered your form, your traveling grain of wheat:

as if clay or wheat field, guitars or clusters of Chillán fruit
realize their places, in you: imposing the will
of the savage moon, they defend their belonging in you.

*D*esnuda eres tan simple como una de tus manos,
lisa, terrestre, mínima, redonda, transparente,
tienes líneas de luna, caminos de manzana,
desnuda eres delgada como el trigo desnudo.

Desnuda eres azul como la noche en Cuba,
tienes enredaderas y estrellas en el pelo,
desnuda eres enorme y amarilla
como el verano en una iglesia de oro.

Desnuda eres pequeña como una de tus uñas,
curva, sutil, rosada hasta que nace el día
y te metes en el subterráneo del mundo

como en un largo túnel de trajes y trabajos:
tu claridad se apaga, se viste, se deshoja
y otra vez vuelve a ser una mano desnuda.

XXVII

Naked, you are simple as one of your hands,
smooth, earthy, small, transparent, round:
you have moon-lines, apple-pathways:
naked, you are slender as a naked grain of wheat.

Naked, you are blue as a night in Cuba;
you have vines and stars in your hair;
naked, you are spacious and yellow
as summer in a golden church.

Naked, you are tiny as one of your nails—
curved, subtle, rosy, till the day is born
and you withdraw to the underground world,

as if down a long tunnel of clothing and of chores:
your clear light dims, gets dressed—drops its leaves—
and becomes a naked hand again.

Amor, de grano a grano, de planeta a planeta,
la red del viento con sus países sombríos,
la guerra con sus zapatos de sangre,
o bien el día y la noche de la espiga.

Por donde fuimos, islas o puentes o banderas,
violines del fugaz otoño acribillado,
repitió la alegría los labios de la copa,
el dolor nos detuvo con su lección de llanto.

En todas las repúblicas desarrollaba el viento
su pabellón impune, su glacial cabellera,
y luego regresaba la flor a sus trabajos.

Pero en nosotros nunca se calcinó el otoño.
Y en nuestra patria inmóvil germinaba y crecía
el amor con los derechos del rocío.

Love, from seed to seed, from planet to planet,
the wind with its net through the darkening nations,
war with its bloody shoes,
or even the day, with a thorny night.

Wherever we went, islands or bridges or flags,
there were the violins of the fleeting autumn, bullet-laced;
happiness echoing at the rim of the wineglass;
sorrow detaining us, with its lesson of tears.

Through all those republics the wind whipped—
its arrogant pavillions, its glacial hair;
it would return the flowers, later, to their work.

But no withering autumn ever touched us.
In our stable place a love sprouted, grew:
as rightfully empowered as the dew.

Vienes de la pobreza de las casas del Sur,
de las regiones duras con frío y terremoto
que cuando hasta sus dioses rodaron a la muerte
nos dieron la lección de la vida en la greda.

Eres un caballito de greda negra, un beso
de barro oscuro, amor, amapola de greda,
paloma del crepúsculo que voló en los caminos,
alcancía con lágrimas de nuestra pobre infancia.

Muchacha, has conservado tu corazón de pobre,
tus pies de pobre acostumbrados a las piedras,
tu boca que no siempre tuvo pan o delicia.

Eres del pobre Sur, de donde viene mi alma:
en su cielo tu madre sigue lavando ropa
con mi madre. Por eso te escogí, compañera.

*Y*ou come from poverty, from the houses of the South,
from the rugged landscapes of cold and of earthquake
that offered us—after those gods had tumbled
to their deaths—the lesson of life, shaped in clay.

You are a little horse of black clay, a kiss
of dark mud, my love, a clay poppy,
dove of the twilight that flew along the roads,
piggy bank of tears from our poor childhood.

Little one, you've kept the heart of poverty in you,
your feet used to sharp rocks,
your mouth that didn't always have bread, or sweets.

You come from the poor South, where my soul began;
in that high sky your mother is still washing clothes
with my mother. That's why I chose you, *compañera*.

*T*ienes del archipiélago las hebras del alerce,
la carne trabajada por los siglos del tiempo,
venas que conocieron el mar de las maderas,
sangre verde caída del cielo a la memoria.

Nadie recogerá mi corazón perdido
entre tantas raíces, en la amarga frescura
del sol multiplicado por la furia del agua,
allí vive la sombra que no viaja conmigo.

Por eso tú saliste del Sur como una isla
poblada y coronada por plumas y maderas
y yo sentí el aroma de los bosques errantes,

hallé la miel oscura que conocí en la selva,
y toqué en tus caderas los pétalos sombríos
que nacieron conmigo y construyeron mi alma.

You have the thick hair of a larch from the archipelago,
skin made by centuries of time,
veins that have known seas of forest timber,
green blood dropped from the sky into memory.

No one will retrieve my lost heart
from all those roots, from the fresh-bitter glare
of the sun multiplied on the water.
That's where it lives, the shadow that does not follow me.

And that's why you rose from the South like an island
crowded and crowned with feathers and timber:
I smelled the scent of those drifting forests,

I found the dark honey I'd known in the woods;
on your hips I touched those opaque petals
that were born with me, that made up my soul.

Con laureles del Sur y orégano de Lota
te corono, pequeña monarca de mis huesos,
y no puede faltarte esa corona
que elabora la tierra con bálsamo y follaje.

Eres, como el que te ama, de las provincias verdes:
de allá trajimos barro que nos corre en la sangre,
en la ciudad andamos, como tantos, perdidos,
temerosos de que cierren el mercado.

Bienamada, tu sombra tiene olor a ciruela,
tus ojos escondieron en el Sur sus raíces,
tu corazón es una paloma de alcancía,

tu cuerpo es liso como las piedras en el agua,
tus besos son racimos con rocío,
y yo a tu lado vivo con la tierra.

Little queen of my bones, I crown you
with laurels from the South and oregano from Lota.
And you cannot do without that crown, which the earth made
for you with balsam and green leaves.

Like the man who loves you, you come from the green
    provinces:
from there we brought the clay that runs in our blood.
In the city we wander like other countrypeople, confused,
afraid the market will shut down before we get there.

Dearest, your shadow has the fragrance of plums;
your eyes set their roots in the South;
your heart is a clay toy shaped like a dove.

Your body is smooth as stones in the water;
your kisses are clusters of fruit, fresh with dew.
As I live by your side, I live with the earth.

La casa en la mañana con la verdad revuelta
de sábanas y plumas, el origen del día
sin dirección, errante como una pobre barca,
entre los horizontes del orden y del sueño.

Las cosas quieren arrastrar vestigios,
adherencias sin rumbo, herencias frías,
los papeles esconden vocales arrugadas
y en la botella el vino quiere seguir su ayer.

Ordenadora, pasas vibrando como abeja
tocando las regiones perdidas por la sombra,
conquistando la luz con tu blanca energía.

Y se construye entonces la claridad de nuevo:
obedecen las cosas al viento de la vida
y el orden establece su pan y su paloma.

*T*he house this morning—with its truths
scrambled, blankets and feathers, the start of the day
already in flux—drifts like a poor little boat
between its horizons of order and of sleep.

Objects want only to drag themselves along:
vestiges, entropic followers, cold legacies.
Papers hide their shriveled vowels;
the wine in the bottle prefers to continue yesterday.

But you—The One Who Puts Things in Order—you shimmer
through like a bee, probing spaces lost to the darkness:
conquering light, you with your white energy.

So you construct a new clarity here,
and objects obey, following the wind of life:
an Order establishes its bread, its dove.

Afternoon / *Mediodía*

Amor, ahora nos vamos a la casa
donde la enredadera sube por las escalas:
antes que llegues tú llegó a tu dormitorio
el verano desnudo con pies de madreselva.

Nuestros besos errantes recorrieron el mundo:
Armenia, espesa gota de miel desenterrada,
Ceylán, paloma verde, y el Yang Tsé separando
con antigua paciencia los días de las noches.

Y ahora, bienamada, por el mar crepitante
volvemos como dos aves ciegas al muro,
al nido de la lejana primavera,

porque el amor no puede volar sin detenerse:
al muro o a las piedras del mar van nuestras vidas,
a nuestro territorio regresaron los besos.

Love, we're going home now,
where the vines clamber over the trellis:
even before you, the summer will arrive,
on its honeysuckle feet, in your bedroom.

Our nomadic kisses wandered over all the world:
Armenia, dollop of disinterred honey—:
Ceylon, green dove—: and the Yang-Tse with its old
old patience, dividing the day from the night.

And now, dearest, we return, across the crackling sea
like two blind birds to their wall,
to their nest in a distant spring:

because love cannot always fly without resting,
our lives return to the wall, to the rocks of the sea:
our kisses head back home where they belong.

Eres hija del mar y prima del orégano,
nadadora, tu cuerpo es de agua pura,
cocinera, tu sangre es tierra viva
y tus costumbres son floridas y terrestres.

Al agua van tus ojos y levantan las olas,
a la tierra tus manos y saltan las semillas,
en agua y tierra tienes propiedades profundas
que en ti se juntan como las leyes de la greda.

Náyade, corta tu cuerpo la turquesa
y luego resurrecto florece en la cocina
de tal modo que asumes cuanto existe

y al fin duermes rodeada por mis brazos que apartan
de la sombra sombría, para que tú descanses,
legumbres, algas, hierbas: la espuma de tus sueños.

You are the daughter of the sea, oregano's first cousin.
Swimmer, your body is pure as the water;
cook, your blood is quick as the soil.
Everything you do is full of flowers, rich with the earth.

Your eyes go out toward the water, and the waves rise;
your hands go out to the earth, and the seeds swell;
you know the deep essence of water and the earth,
conjoined in you like a formula for clay.

Naiad: cut your body into turquoise pieces,
they will bloom resurrected in the kitchen.
This is how you become everything that lives.

And so, at last, you sleep, in the circle of my arms
that push back the shadows so that you can rest—
vegetables, seaweed, herbs: the foam of your dreams.

*T*u mano fue volando de mis ojos al día.
Entró la luz como un rosal abierto.
Arena y cielo palpitaban como una
culminante colmena cortada en las turquesas.

Tu mano tocó sílabas que tintineaban, copas,
alcuzas con aceites amarillos,
corolas, manantiales y, sobre todo, amor,
amor: tu mano pura preservó las cucharas.

La tarde fue. La noche deslizó sigilosa
sobre el sueño del hombre su cápsula celeste.
Un triste olor salvaje soltó la madreselva.

Y tu mano volvió de su vuelo volando
a cerrar su plumaje que yo creí perdido
sobre mis ojos devorados por la sombra.

Your hand flew from my eyes into the day.
The light arrived and opened like a rose garden.
Sand and sky throbbed like an ultimate
beehive carved in the turquoise.

Your hand touched syllables that rang like bells,
touched cups, barrels full of yellow oil,
flower petals, fountains, and, above all, love,
Love: your pure hand guarded the ladles.

The afternoon . . . was. Quietly the night slid
over a man asleep, its celestial capsule.
Honeysuckle set loose its sad savage odor.

And then your hand fluttered, it flew back again:
it closed its wings, its feathers I had thought were lost,
over my eyes the darkness had swallowed.

Corazón mío, reina del apio y de la artesa:
pequeña leoparda del hilo y la cebolla:
me gusta ver brillar tu imperio diminuto,
las armas de la cera, del vino, del aceite,

del ajo, de la tierra por tus manos abierta
de la sustancia azul encendida en tus manos,
de la transmigración del sueño a la ensalada,
del reptil enrollado en la manguera.

Tú, con tu podadora levantando el perfume,
tú, con la dirección del jabón en la espuma,
tú, subiendo mis locas escalas y escaleras,

tú, manejando el síntoma de mi caligrafía
y encontrando en la arena del cuaderno
las letras extraviadas que buscaban tu boca.

My heart, queen of the beehive and the barnyard,
little leopard of the string and the onions,
I love to watch your miniature empire
sparkle: your weapons of wax and wine and oil,

garlic, and the soil that opens for your hands,
the blue material that ignites in your hands,
the transmigration of dream into salad,
the snake rolled up in the garden hose.

You with your sickle that lifts the perfumes,
you with the bossy soapsuds,
you climbing my crazy ladders and stairs.

You taking charge: even my handwriting, its characteristics,
even the sand grains in my notebooks—finding in those pages
lost syllables that were searching for your mouth.

Oh amor, oh rayo loco y amenaza purpúrea,
me visitas y subes por tu fresca escalera
el castillo que el tiempo coronó de neblinas,
las pálidas paredes del corazón cerrado.

Nadie sabrá que sólo fue la delicadeza
construyendo cristales duros como ciudades
y que la sangre abría túneles desdichados
sin que su monarquía derribara el invierno.

Por eso, amor, tu boca, tu piel, tu luz, tus penas,
fueron el patrimonio de la vida, los dones
sagrados de la lluvia, de la naturaleza

que recibe y levanta la gravidez del grano,
la tempestad secreta del vino en las bodegas,
la llamarada del cereal en el suelo.

O love, O crazy sunbeam and purple premonition,
you come to me and climb your cool stairway,
the castle that time has crowned with fog,
pale walls of a closed heart.

No one else will know that only a delicacy could do it,
building its crystals as strong as a city;
that the blood poured open its sad tunnels, but its strength
never did overpower the winter. Love,

that is why your mouth, your skin, your light, your sadnesses
were all the patrimony of life, the blessed
gift of the rain, of the natural world

that holds and lifts the pregnant seeds,
the secret storm of the wine in the cellars,
the flare of the corn in the soil.

Tu casa suena como un tren a mediodía,
zumban las avispas, cantan las cacerolas,
la cascada enumera los hechos del rocío,
tu risa desarrolla su trino de palmera.

La luz azul del muro conversa con la piedra,
llega como un pastor silbando un telegrama
y entre las dos higueras de voz verde
Homero sube con zapatos sigilosos.

Sólo aquí la ciudad no tiene voz ni llanto,
ni sinfín, ni sonatas, ni labios, ni bocina,
sino un discurso de cascada y de leones,

y tú que subes, cantas, corres, caminas, bajas,
plantas, coses, cocinas, clavas, escribes, vuelves,
o te has ido y se sabe que comenzó el invierno.

Your house sounds like a train at noon:
bees hum, pots sing,
the waterfall catalogues what the soft rain did,
your laugh spins out its trill like a palm tree.

Arriving like a country boy with a singing telegram,
the blue light of the wall talks with the rocks, and there—
climbing the hill, between the two fig trees, with the green
    voice—
comes Homer in his quiet sandals.

Only here the city has no voice, no mouth, nothing so
relentless, no sonatas, shouts or car horns: here,
instead, a quiet collocation of waterfalls and lions

and you—who rises, sings, runs, walks, bends,
plants, sews, cooks, hammers, writes, returns—
or have you gone away—?— (then I'd know the winter had
    begun).

Pero olvidé que tus manos satisfacían
las raíces, regando rosas enmarañadas,
hasta que florecieron tus huellas digitales
en la plenaria paz de la naturaleza.

El azadón y el agua como animales tuyos
te acompañan, mordiendo y lamiendo la tierra,
y es así cómo, trabajando, desprendes
fecundidad, fogosa frescura de claveles.

Amor y honor de abejas pido para tus manos
que en la tierra confunden su estirpe transparente,
y hasta en mi corazón abren su agricultura,

de tal modo que soy como piedra quemada
que de pronto, contigo, canta, porque recibe
el agua de los bosques por tu voz conducida.

*B*ut I forgot that your hands fed the roots,
watering the tangled roses,
till your fingerprints bloomed
full, in a natural peace.

Like pets, your hoe and your sprinkling can
follow you around, biting and licking the earth.
That work is how you let this richness loose,
the carnations' fiery freshness.

I wish the love and dignity of bees for your hands,
mixing and spreading their transparent brood
in the earth: they cultivate even my heart,

so that I am like a scorched rock
that suddenly sings when you are near, because it drinks
the water you carry from the forest, in your voice.

Era verde el silencio, mojada era la luz,
temblaba el mes de junio como una mariposa
y en el austral dominio, desde el mar y las piedras,
Matilde, atravesaste el mediodía.

Ibas cargada de flores ferruginosas,
algas que el viento sur atormenta y olvida,
aún blancas, agrietadas por la sal devorante,
tus manos levantaban las espigas de arena.

Amo tus dones puros, tu piel de piedra intacta,
tus uñas ofrecidas en el sol de tus dedos,
tu boca derramada por toda la alegría,

pero, para mi casa vecina del abismo,
dame el atormentado sistema del silencio,
el pabellón del mar olvidado en la arena.

It was green, the silence; the light was moist;
the month of June trembled like a butterfly;
and you, Matilde, passed through noon,
through the regions of the South, the sea and the stones.

You went carrying your cargo of iron flowers,
seaweed battered and abandoned by the South wind,
but your hands, still white, cracked by corrosive salt,
gathered the blooming stalks that grew in the sand.

I love your pure gifts, your skin like whole stones,
your nails, offerings, in the suns of your fingers,
your mouth brimming with all joys.

Oh, in my house beside the abyss, give me
the tormenting structure of that silence,
pavillion of the sea, forgotten in the sand.

Desdichas del mes de enero cuando el indiferente
mediodía establece su ecuación en el cielo,
un oro duro como el vino de una copa colmada
llena la tierra hasta sus límites azules.

Desdichas de este tiempo parecidas a uvas
pequeñas que agruparon verde amargo,
confusas, escondidas lágrimas de los días,
hasta que la intemperie publicó sus racimos.

Sí, gérmenes, dolores, todo lo que palpita
aterrado, a la luz crepitante de enero,
madurará, arderá como ardieron los frutos.

Divididos serán los pesares: el alma
dará un golpe de viento, y la morada
quedará limpia con el pan fresco en la mesa.

January rough times, when the indifferent
noon makes its equation in the sky.
Like wine in a glass, a hard gold
fills the earth to its blue limits.

Rough times of the season, like little grapes
distilling green bitterness,
the hidden confused tears of the days, swelling
in clusters, till bad weather lays them bare.

Yes: seed-germs, and grief, and everything that throbs
frightened in the crackling January light
will ripen, will burn, as the fruit burned ripe.

And our problems will crumble apart, the soul
blow through like a wind, and here where we live
will all be clean again, with fresh bread on the table.

*R*adiantes días balanceados por el agua marina,
concentrados como el interior de una piedra amarilla
cuyo esplendor de miel no derribó el desorden:
preservó su pureza de rectángulo.

Crepita, sí, la hora como fuego o abejas
y es verde la tarea de sumergirse en hojas,
hasta que hacia la altura es el follaje
un mundo centelleante que se apaga y susurra.

Sed del fuego, abrasadora multitud del estío
que construye un Edén con unas cuantas hojas,
porque la tierra de rostro oscuro no quiere sufrimientos

sino frescura o fuego, agua o pan para todos,
y nada debería dividir a los hombres
sino el sol o la noche, la luna o las espigas.

Radiant days rolling on the water, intense as the inside
of a yellow rock, its splendor like honey:
that wasn't damaged by all the turmoil.
That kept its four-square purity.

Yes: the daylight crackles like a fire, or like bees,
getting on with its green work, burying itself in leaves:
till up at the top the foliage reaches
a bright world that flickers and whispers.

Thirst of fire, scorch and multitudinousness of summer,
which builds an Eden with a few green leaves—:
because the dark-faced earth does not want suffering;

it wants freshness—fire—water—bread, for everyone:
nothing should separate people
but the sun or the night, the moon or the branches.

*U*n signo tuyo busco en todas las otras,
en el brusco, ondulante río de las mujeres,
trenzas, ojos apenas sumergidos,
pies claros que resbalan navegando en la espuma.

De pronto me parece que diviso tus uñas
oblongas, fugitivas, sobrinas de un cerezo,
y otra vez es tu pelo que pasa y me parece
ver arder en el agua tu retrato de hoguera.

Miré, pero ninguna llevaba tu latido,
tu luz, la greda oscura que trajiste del bosque,
ninguna tuvo tus diminutas orejas.

Tú eres total y breve, de todas eres una,
y así contigo voy recorriendo y amando
un ancho Misisipí de estuario femenino.

XLIII

I hunt for a sign of you in all the others,
in the rapid undulant river of women,
braids, shyly sinking eyes,
light step that slides, sailing through the foam.

Suddenly I think I can make out your nails—
oblong, quick, nieces of a cherry—:
then it's your hair that passes by, and I think
I see your image, a bonfire, burning in the water.

I searched, but no one else had your rhythms,
your light, the shady day you brought from the forest;
nobody had your tiny ears.

You are whole—exact—and everything you are is one,
and so I go along, with you I float along, loving
a wide Mississippi toward a feminine sea.

S abrás que no te amo y que te amo
puesto que de dos modos es la vida,
la palabra es un ala del silencio,
el fuego tiene una mitad de frío.

Yo te amo para comenzar a amarte,
para recomenzar el infinito
y para no dejar de amarte nunca:
por eso no te amo todavía.

Te amo y no te amo como si tuviera
en mis manos las llaves de la dicha
y un incierto destino desdichado.

Mi amor tiene dos vidas para amarte.
Por eso te amo cuando no te amo
y por eso te amo cuando te amo.

XLIV

You must know that I do not love *and* that I love you,
because everything alive has its two sides;
a word is one wing of the silence,
fire has its cold half.

I love you in order to begin to love you,
to start infinity again
and never to stop loving you:
that's why I do not love you yet.

I love you, and I do not love you, as if I held
keys in my hand: to a future of joy—
a wretched, muddled fate—

My love has two lives, in order to love you:
that's why I love you when I do not love you,
and also why I love you when I do.

No estés lejos de mí un solo día, porque cómo,
porque, no sé decirlo, es largo el día,
y te estaré esperando como en las estaciones
cuando en alguna parte se durmieron los trenes.

No te vayas por una hora porque entonces
en esa hora se juntan las gotas del desvelo
y tal vez todo el humo que anda buscando casa
venga a matar aún mi corazón perdido.

Ay que no se quebrante tu silueta en la arena,
ay que no vuelen tus párpados en la ausencia:
no te vayas por un minuto, bienamada,

porque en ese minuto te habrás ido tan lejos
que yo cruzaré toda la tierra preguntando
si volverás o si me dejarás muriendo.

*D*on't go far off, not even for a day, because—
because—I don't know how to say it: a day is long
and I will be waiting for you, as in an empty station
when the trains are parked off somewhere else, asleep.

Don't leave me, even for an hour, because
then the little drops of anguish will all run together,
the smoke that roams looking for a home will drift
into me, choking my lost heart.

Oh, may your silhouette never dissolve on the beach;
may your eyelids never flutter into the empty distance.
Don't leave me for a second, my dearest,

because in that moment you'll have gone so far
I'll wander mazily over all the earth, asking,
Will you come back? Will you leave me here, dying?

De las estrellas que admiré, mojadas
por ríos y rocíos diferentes,
yo no escogí sino la que yo amaba
y desde entonces duermo con la noche.

De la ola, una ola y otra ola,
verde mar, verde frío, rama verde,
yo no escogí sino una sola ola:
la ola indivisible de tu cuerpo.

Todas las gotas, todas las raíces,
todos los hilos de la luz vinieron,
me vinieron a ver tarde o temprano.

Yo quise para mí tu cabellera.
Y de todos los dones de mi patria
sólo escogí tu corazón salvaje.

Of all the stars I admired, drenched
in various rivers and mists,
I chose only the one I love.
Since then I sleep with the night.

Of all the waves, one wave and another wave,
green sea, green chill, branchings of green,
I chose only the one wave,
the indivisible wave of your body.

All the waterdrops, all the roots,
all the threads of light gathered to me here;
they came to me sooner or later.

I wanted your hair, all for myself.
From all the graces my homeland offered
I chose only your savage heart.

Detrás de mí en la rama quiero verte.
Poco a poco te convertiste en fruto.
No te costó subir de las raíces
cantando con tu sílaba de savia.

Y aquí estarás primero en flor fragante,
en la estatua de un beso convertida,
hasta que sol y tierra, sangre y cielo,
te otorguen la delicia y la dulzura.

En la rama veré tu cabellera,
tu signo madurando en el follaje,
acercando las hojas a mi sed,

y llenará mi boca tu substancia,
el beso que subió desde la tierra
con tu sangre de fruta enamorada.

I want to look back and see you in the branches.
Little by little you turned into fruit.
It was easy for you to rise from the roots,
singing your syllable of sap.

Here you will be a fragrant flower first,
changed to the statuesque form of a kiss,
till the sun and the earth, blood and the sky, fulfill
their promises of sweetness and pleasure, in you.

There in the branches I will recognize your hair,
your image ripening in the leaves,
bringing the petals nearer my thirst,

and my mouth will fill with the taste of you,
the kiss that rose from the earth
with your blood, the blood of a lover's fruit.

Dos amantes dichosos hacen un solo pan,
una sola gota de luna en la hierba,
dejan andando dos sombras que se reúnen,
dejan un solo sol vacío en una cama.

De todas las verdades escogieron el día:
no se ataron con hilos sino con un aroma,
y no despedazaron la paz ni las palabras.
La dicha es una torre transparente.

El aire, el vino van con los dos amantes,
la noche les regala sus pétalos dichosos,
tienen derecho a todos los claveles.

Dos amantes dichosos no tienen fin ni muerte,
nacen y mueren muchas veces mientras viven,
tienen la eternidad de la naturaleza.

*T*wo happy lovers make one bread,
a single moon drop in the grass.
Walking, they cast two shadows that flow together;
waking, they leave one sun empty in their bed.

Of all the possible truths, they chose the day;
they held it, not with ropes but with an aroma.
They did not shred the peace; they did not shatter words;
their happiness is a transparent tower.

The air and wine accompany the lovers.
The night delights them with its joyous petals.
They have a right to all the carnations.

Two happy lovers, without an ending, with no death,
they are born, they die, many times while they live:
they have the eternal life of the Natural.

Es hoy: todo el ayer se fue cayendo
entre dedos de luz y ojos de sueño,
mañana llegará con pasos verdes:
nadie detiene el río de la aurora.

Nadie detiene el río de tus manos,
los ojos de tu sueño, bienamada,
eres temblor del tiempo que transcurre
entre luz vertical y sol sombrío,

y el cielo cierra sobre ti sus alas
llevándote y trayéndote a mis brazos
con puntual, misteriosa cortesía:

Por eso canto al día y a la luna,
al mar, al tiempo, a todos los planetas,
a tu voz diurna y a tu piel nocturna.

It's today: all of yesterday dropped away
among the fingers of the light and the sleeping eyes.
Tomorrow will come on its green footsteps;
no one can stop the river of the dawn.

No one can stop the river of your hands,
your eyes and their sleepiness, my dearest.
You are the trembling of time, which passes
between the vertical light and the darkening sky.

The sky folds its wings over you,
lifting you, carrying you to my arms
with its punctual, mysterious courtesy.

That's why I sing to the day and to the moon,
to the sea, to time, to all the planets,
to your daily voice, to your nocturnal skin.

Cotapos dice que tu risa cae
como un halcón desde una brusca torre
y, es verdad, atraviesas el follaje del mundo
con un solo relámpago de tu estirpe celeste

que cae, y corta, y saltan las lenguas del rocío,
las aguas del diamante, la luz con sus abejas
y allí donde vivía con su barba el silencio
estallan las granadas del sol y las estrellas,

se viene abajo el cielo con la noche sombría,
arden a plena luna campanas y claveles,
y corren los caballos de los talabarteros:

porque tú siendo tan pequeñita como eres
dejas caer la risa desde tu meteoro
electrizando el nombre de la naturaleza.

Cotapos says your laughter drops
like a hawk from a stony tower. It's true:
daughter of the sky, you slit the world
and its green leaves, with one bolt of your lightning:

it falls, it thunders: the tongues of the dew,
the waters of a diamond, the light with its bees
leap. And there where a long-bearded silence had lived,
little bombs of light explode, the sun and the stars,

down comes the sky, with its thick-shadowed night,
bells and carnations glow in the full moon,
the saddlemakers' horses gallop.

Because you are small as you are, let it
rip: let the meteor of your laughter
fly: electrify the natural names of things!

Tu risa pertenece a un árbol entreabierto
por un rayo, por un relámpago plateado
que desde el cielo cae quebrándose en la copa,
partiendo en dos el árbol con una sola espada.

Sólo en las tierras altas de follaje con nieve
nace una risa como la tuya, bienamante,
es la risa del aire desatado en la altura,
costumbres de araucaria, bienamada.

Cordillerana mía, chillaneja evidente,
corta con los cuchillos de tu risa la sombra,
la noche, la mañana, la miel del mediodía,

y que salten al cielo las aves del follaje
cuando como una luz derrochadora
rompe tu risa el árbol de la vida.

Your laugh: it reminds me of a tree
fissured by a lightning streak, by a silver bolt
that drops from the sky, splitting the poll,
slicing the tree with its sword.

A laugh like yours I love is born
only in the foliage and snow of the highlands,
the air's laugh that bursts loose in those altitudes,
dearest: the Araucanian tradition.

O my mountain woman, my clear Chillán volcano,
slash your laughter through the shadows,
the night, morning, honey of the noon:

birds of the foliage will leap in the air
when your laugh like an extravagant
light breaks through the tree of life.

Cantas, y a sol y a cielo con tu canto
tu voz desgrana el cereal del día,
hablan los pinos con su lengua verde:
trinan todas las aves del invierno.

El mar llena sus sótanos de pasos,
de campanas, cadenas y gemidos,
tintinean metales y utensilios,
suenan las ruedas de la caravana.

Pero sólo tu voz escucho y sube
tu voz con vuelo y precisión de flecha,
baja tu voz con gravedad de lluvia,

tu voz esparce altísimas espadas,
vuelve tu voz cargada de violetas
y luego me acompaña por el cielo.

*Y*ou sing, and your voice peels the husk
of the day's grain, your song with the sun and sky,
the pine trees speak with their green tongue:
all the birds of the winter whistle.

The sea fills its cellar with footfalls,
with bells, chains, whimpers,
the tools and the metals jangle,
wheels of the caravan creak.

But I hear only your voice, your voice
soars with the zing and precision of an arrow,
it drops with the gravity of rain,

your voice scatters the highest swords
and returns with its cargo of violets:
it accompanies me through the sky.

*A*quí está el pan, el vino, la mesa, la morada:
el menester del hombre, la mujer y la vida:
a este sitio corría la paz vertiginosa,
por esta luz ardió la común quemadura.

Honor a tus dos manos que vuelan preparando
los blancos resultados del canto y la cocina,
salve! la integridad de tus pies corredores,
viva! la bailarina que baila con la escoba.

Aquellos bruscos ríos con aguas y amenazas,
aquel atormentado pabellón de la espuma,
aquellos incendiarios panales y arrecifes

son hoy este reposo de tu sangre en la mía,
este cauce estrellado y azul como la noche,
esta simplicidad sin fin de la ternura.

Here are the bread—the wine—the table—the house:
a man's needs, and a woman's, and a life's.
Peace whirled through and settled in this place:
the common fire burned, to make this light.

Hail to your two hands, which fly and make
their white creations, the singing and the food:
salve! the wholesomeness of your busy feet;
viva! the ballerina who dances with the broom.

Those rugged rivers of water and of threat,
torturous pavillions of the foam,
incendiary hives and reefs: today

they are this respite, your blood in mine,
this path, starry and blue as the night,
this never-ending simple tenderness.

Evening / *Tarde*

Espléndida razón, demonio claro
del racimo absoluto, del recto mediodía,
aquí estamos al fin, sin soledad y solos,
lejos del desvarío de la ciudad salvaje.

Cuando la línea pura rodea su paloma
y el fuego condecora la paz con su alimento
tú y yo erigimos este celeste resultado.
Razón y amor desnudos viven en esta casa.

Sueños furiosos, ríos de amarga certidumbre,
decisiones más duras que el sueño de un martillo
cayeron en la doble copa de los amantes.

Hasta que en la balanza se elevaron, gemelos,
la razón y el amor como dos alas.
Así se construyó la transparencia.

*L*uminous mind, bright devil
of absolute clusterings, of the upright noon—:
here we are at last, alone, without loneliness,
far from the savage city's delirium.

Just as a pure line describes the dove's curve,
as the fire honors and nourishes peace,
so you and I made this heavenly outcome.
The mind and love live naked in this house.

Furious dreams, rivers of bitter certainty,
decisions harder than the dreams of a hammer
flowed into the lovers' double cup,

until those twins were lifted into balance
on the scale: the mind and love, like two wings.
—So this transparency was built.

Espinas, vidrios rotos, enfermedades, llanto
asedian día y noche la miel de los felices
y no sirve la torre, ni el viaje, ni los muros:
la desdicha atraviesa la paz de los dormidos,

el dolor sube y baja y acerca sus cucharas
y no hay hombre sin este movimiento,
no hay natalicio, no hay techo ni cercado:
hay que tomar en cuenta este atributo.

Y en el amor no valen tampoco ojos cerrados,
profundos lechos lejos del pestilente herido,
o del que paso a paso conquista su bandera.

Porque la vida pega como cólera o río
y abre un túnel sangriento por donde nos vigilan
los ojos de una inmensa familia de dolores.

Thorns, shattered glass, sickness, crying: all day
they attack the honied contentment. And neither the tower,
nor the walls, nor secret passageways are of much help.
Trouble seeps through, into the sleepers' peace.

Sorrow rises and falls, comes near with its deep spoons,
and no one can live without this endless motion;
without it there would be no birth, no roof, no fence.
It happens: we have to account for it.

Eyes squeezed shut in love don't help,
nor soft beds far from the pestilent sick,
from the conquerer who advances, pace by pace, with his flag.

For life throbs like a bile, like a river: it opens
a bloody tunnel where eyes stare through at us,
the eyes of a huge and sorrowful family.

*A*costúmbrate a ver detrás de mí la sombra
y que tus manos salgan del rencor, transparentes,
como si en la mañana del mar fueran creadas:
la sal te dio, amor mío, proporción cristalina.

La envidia sufre, muere, se agota con mi canto.
Uno a uno agonizan sus tristes capitanes.
Yo digo amor, y el mundo se puebla de palomas.
Cada sílaba mía trae la primavera.

Entonces tú, florida, corazón, bienamada,
sobre mis ojos como los follajes del cielo
eres, y yo te miro recostada en la tierra.

Veo el sol trasmigrar racimos a tu rostro,
mirando hacia la altura reconozco tus pasos.
Matilde, bienamada, diadema, bienvenida!

Get used to seeing the shadow behind me, accept
that your hands will emerge clean from the rancor
as if they were made in the morning of the river.
My love, the salt gave you its crystalline proportions.

Envy suffers, expires, my songs exhaust it;
one by one its sad captains agonize and die.
I say *love*, and the world fills with doves.
Each syllable of mine makes the spring arrive.

Then there you are—in bloom, my heart, my dearest:
over my eyes like the leaves of the sky,
there you are. I look at you, lying on the earth.

I see the sun bring its buds to your face;
looking up at the heavens I recognize your steps.
O Matilde, my dearest, crown of glory: welcome!

*M*ienten los que dijeron que yo perdí la luna,
los que profetizaron mi porvenir de arena,
aseveraron tantas cosas con lenguas frías:
quisieron prohibir la flor del universo.

"Ya no cantará más el ámbar insurgente
de la sirena, no tiene sino pueblo."
Y masticaban sus incesantes papeles
patrocinando para mi guitarra el olvido.

Yo les lancé a los ojos las lanzas deslumbrantes
de nuestro amor clavando tu corazón y el mío,
yo reclamé el jazmín que dejaban tus huellas,

yo me perdí de noche sin luz bajo tus párpados
y cuando me envolvió la claridad
nací de nuevo, dueño de mi propia tiniebla.

They're liars, those who say I lost the moon,
who foretold a future like a public desert for me,
who gossiped so much with their cold tongues:
they tried to ban the flower of the universe.

"The quick spontaneous mermaids' amber
is finished. Now he has only the people."
And they gnawed on their incessant papers,
they plotted an oblivion for my guitar.

But I tossed—ha! into their eyes!—the dazzling lances
of our love, piercing your heart and mine.
I gathered the jasmine your footsteps left behind.

I got lost in the night, without the light
of your eyelids, and when the night surrounded me
I was born again: I was the owner of my own darkness.

Entre los espadones de fierro literario
paso yo como un marinero remoto
que no conoce las esquinas y que canta
porque sí, porque cómo si no fuera por eso.

De los atormentados archipiélagos traje
mi acordeón con borrascas, rachas de lluvia loca,
y una costumbre lenta de cosas naturales:
ellas determinaron mi corazón silvestre.

Así cuando los dientes de la literatura
trataron de morder mis honrados talones,
yo pasé, sin saber, cantando con el viento

hacia los almacenes lluviosos de mi infancia,
hacia los bosques fríos del Sur indefinible,
hacia donde mi vida se llenó con tu aroma.

Among the broadswords of literary iron
I wander like a foreign sailor, who does not know
the streets, or their angles, and who sings because
that's how it is, because if not for that what else is there?

From the stormy archipelagoes I brought
my windy accordion, waves of crazy rain,
the habitual slowness of natural things:
they made up my wild heart.

And so when the sharp little teeth of Literature
snapped at my honest heels, I passed along
unsuspectingly, singing with the wind,

toward the rainy dockyards of my childhood,
toward the cool forests of the indefinable South,
toward where my heart was filled with your fragrance.

(G. M.)

Pobres poetas a quienes la vida y la muerte
persiguieron con la misma tenacidad sombría
y luego son cubiertos por impasible pompa,
entregados al rito y al diente funerario.

Ellos—oscuros como piedrecitas—ahora
detrás de los caballos arrogantes, tendidos
van, gobernados al fin por los intrusos,
entre los edecanes, a dormir sin silencio.

Antes y ya seguros de que está muerto el muerto
hacen de las exequias un festín miserable
con pavos, puercos y otros oradores.

Acecharon su muerte y entonces la ofendieron:
sólo porque su boca está cerrada
y ya no puede contestar su canto.

(*G. M.*)

*P*oor unlucky poets: whom both life and death
harass, with the same dark stubbornness,
who then are smothered in mindless pomp, committed
to rituals, to a funeral like a craw full of teeth.

Obscure as pebbles now, they are dragged
behind the arrogant horses, to sleep
without silence, overcome in the end
by the invaders, among their minions—

who, then, certain the dead one *is* dead, once and for all,
celebrate their sniveling feast at his funeral
with turkeys, and pigs, and other orators.

They sabotaged his death, and now they defame it—
but only because his mouth is shut:
he can no longer protest with his song.

A ti te hiere aquel que quiso hacerme daño,
y el golpe del veneno contra mí dirigido
como por una red pasa entre mis trabajos
y en ti deja una mancha de óxido y desvelo.

No quiero ver, amor, en la luna florida
de tu frente cruzar el odio que me acecha.
No quiero que en tu sueño deje el rencor ajeno
olvidada su inútil corona de cuchillos.

Donde voy van detrás de mí pasos amargos,
donde río una mueca de horror copia mi cara,
donde canto la envidia maldice, ríe y roe.

Y es ésa, amor, la sombra que la vida me ha dado:
es un traje vacío que me sigue cojeando
como un espantapájaros de sonrisa sangrienta.

Those who wanted to wound me wounded you,
and the dose of secret poison meant for me
like a net passes through my work—but leaves
its smear of rust and sleeplessness on you.

I don't want the hate that sabotaged me, Love,
to shadow your forehead's flowering moon;
I don't want some stupid random rancor
to drop its crown of knives onto your dream.

Bitter footsteps follow me;
a hideous grimace mocks my smile; envy spits
a curse, guffaws, gnashes its teeth where I sing.

And that, Love, is the shadow life has given me:
an empty suit of clothes that chases me,
limping, like a scarecrow with a bloody grin.

*T*rajo el amor su cola de dolores,
su largo rayo estático de espinas,
y cerramos los ojos porque nada,
porque ninguna herida nos separe.

No es culpa de tus ojos este llanto:
tus manos no clavaron esta espada:
no buscaron tus pies este camino:
llegó a tu corazón la miel sombría.

Cuando el amor como una inmensa ola
nos estrelló contra la piedra dura,
nos amasó con una sola harina,

cayó el dolor sobre otro dulce rostro
y así en la luz de la estación abierta
se consagró la primavera herida.

$\mathcal{L}$ove dragged its tail of pain,
its train of static thorns behind it,
and we closed our eyes so that nothing,
so that no wound could divide us.

This crying, it's not your eyes' fault;
your hands didn't plunge that sword;
your feet didn't seek this path;
this somber honey found its own way to your heart.

When love like a huge wave
carried us, crashed us against the boulder,
it milled us to a single flour;

this sorrow fell into another, sweeter, face:
so in an open season of the light
this wounded springtime was blessed.

Ay de mí, ay de nosotros, bienamada,
sólo quisimos sólo amor, amarnos,
y entre tantos dolores se dispuso
sólo a nosotros dos ser malheridos.

Quisimos el tú y yo para nosotros,
el tú del beso, el yo del pan secreto,
y así era todo, eternamente simple,
hasta que el odio entró por la ventana.

Odian los que no amaron nuestro amor,
ni ningún otro amor, desventurados
como las sillas de un salón perdido,

hasta que se enredaron en ceniza
y el rostro amenazante que tuvieron
se apagó en el crepúsculo apagado.

Woe is me, woe is us, my dearest:
we wanted only love, to love one another,
but among so many griefs it was fated
that only we two would be so hurt.

We wanted the *you* and the *me* for ourselves,
the *you* of a kiss, the *me* of a secret bread:
and that's how it was, infinitely simple,
till hatred came in through the window.

They *hate*, those who did not love
our love, nor any other love: those people,
wretched as chairs in an empty room—

till they were tangled in ashes,
till their ominous faces
faded in the fading twilight.

*N*o sólo por las tierras desiertas donde la piedra salina
es como la única rosa, la flor por el mar enterrada,
anduve, sino por la orilla de ríos que cortan la nieve.
Las amargas alturas de las cordilleras conocen mis pasos.

Enmarañada, silbante región de mi patria salvaje,
lianas cuyo beso mortal se encadena en la selva,
lamento mojado del ave que surge lanzando sus escalofríos,
oh región de perdidos dolores y llanto inclemente!

No sólo son míos la piel venenosa del cobre
o el salitre extendido como estatua yacente y nevada,
sino la viña, el cerezo premiado por la primavera,

son míos, y yo pertenezco como átomo negro
a las áridas tierras y a la luz del otoño en las uvas,
a esta patria metálica elevada por torres de nieve.

I walked: not only through the wasteland where the
   salted rock is
like the only rose, a flower buried in the sea—
but also on the banks of rivers gouging through the snow;
the high bitter mountain ranges felt my footsteps too.

Tangled, whistling realms of my savage homeland,
liana vines whose deadly kiss is chained to the jungle,
wet cry of the bird that rises, throwing off its shivers:
O realm of lost sorrow and inclement tears!

The poisonous skin of the copper, the nitrate salt spread out
like a statue, crumbled and snowy: they're mine, but not
only them: also the vineyards, the cherries the spring rewards,

they are mine too, and I belong to them, like a black atom
in the arid land, in the autumn light on the grapes,
in this metallic homeland lifted by towers of snow.

De tanto amor mi vida se tiñó de violeta
y fui de rumbo en rumbo como las aves ciegas
hasta llegar a tu ventana, amiga mía:
tú sentiste un rumor de corazón quebrado

y allí de las tinieblas me levanté a tu pecho,
sin ser y sin saber fui a la torre del trigo,
surgí para vivir entre tus manos,
me levanté del mar a tu alegría.

Nadie puede contar lo que te debo, es lúcido
lo que te debo, amor, y es como una raíz
natal de Araucanía, lo que te debo, amada.

Es sin duda estrellado todo lo que te debo,
lo que te debo es como el pozo de una zona silvestre
en donde guardó el tiempo relámpagos errantes.

My life was tinted purple by so much love,
and I veered helter-skelter like a blinded bird
till I reached your window, my friend:
you heard the murmur of a broken heart.

There from the shadows I rose to your breast:
without being or knowing, I flew up the towers of wheat,
I surged to life in your hands,
I rose from the sea to your joy.

No one can reckon what I owe you, Love,
what I owe you is lucid, it is like a root
from Arauco, what I owe you, Love.

Clearly, it is like a star, all that I owe you,
what I owe you is like a well in a wilderness
where time watches over the wandering lightning.

Matilde, dónde estás? Noté, hacia abajo,
entre corbata y corazón, arriba,
cierta melancolía intercostal:
era que tú de pronto eras ausente.

Me hizo falta la luz de tu energía
y miré devorando la esperanza,
miré el vacío que es sin ti una casa,
no quedan sino trágicas ventanas.

De puro taciturno el techo escucha
caer antiguas lluvias deshojadas,
plumas, lo que la noche aprisionó:

y así te espero como casa sola
y volverás a verme y habitarme.
De otro modo me duelen las ventanas.

Matilde, where are you? Down there I noticed,
under my necktie and just above the heart,
a certain pang of grief between the ribs,
you were gone that quickly.

I needed the light of your energy,
I looked around, devouring hope.
I watched the void without you that is like a house,
nothing left but tragic windows.

Out of sheer taciturnity the ceiling listens
to the fall of the ancient leafless rain,
to feathers, to whatever the night imprisoned:

so I wait for you like a lonely house
till you will see me again and live in me.
Till then my windows ache.

*N*o te quiero sino porque te quiero
y de quererte a no quererte llego
y de esperarte cuando no te espero
pasa mi corazón del frío al fuego.

Te quiero sólo porque a ti te quiero,
te odio sin fin, y odiándote te ruego,
y la medida de mi amor viajero
es no verte y amarte como un ciego.

Tal vez consumirá la luz de enero,
su rayo cruel, mi corazón entero,
robándome la llave del sosiego.

En esta historia sólo yo me muero
y moriré de amor porque te quiero,
porque te quiero, amor, a sangre y fuego.

*J*do not love you—except because I love you;
I go from loving to not loving you,
from waiting to not waiting for you
my heart moves from the cold into

the fire. I love you only because it's you
I love; I hate you no end, and hating you
bend to you, and the measure of my changing love for you
is that I do not see you but love you

blindly. Maybe the January light will consume
my heart with its cruel
ray, stealing my key to true

calm. In this part of the story I am the one who
dies, the only one, and I will die of love because I love you,
because I love you, Love, in fire and in blood.

LXVII

*L*a gran lluvia del sur cae sobre Isla Negra
como una sola gota transparente y pesada,
el mar abre sus hojas frías y la recibe,
la tierra aprende el húmedo destino de una copa.

Alma mía, dame en tus besos el agua
salobre de estos meses, la miel del territorio,
la fragancia mojada por mil labios del cielo,
la paciencia sagrada del mar en el invierno.

Algo nos llama, todas las puertas se abren solas,
relata el agua un largo rumor a las ventanas,
crece el cielo hacia abajo tocando las raíces,

y así teje y desteje su red celeste el día
con tiempo, sal, susurros, crecimientos, caminos,
una mujer, un hombre, y el invierno en la tierra.

The great rain from the South falls on Isla Negra
like a single drop, lucid and heavy,
the sea opens its cool leaves and receives it,
the earth learns how a wineglass fulfills

its wet destiny. In your kisses, my soul, give me the water,
salty from these months, the honey of the fields,
fragrance dampened by the sky's thousand lips,
the sacred patience of the sea in winter.

Something calls to us, all the doors turn
open by themselves, the rain repeats its rumor to the windows,
the sky grows downward till it touches the roots:

so the day weaves and unweaves its heavenly net,
with time, salt, whispers, growth, roads,
a woman, a man, and winter on the earth.

LXVIII

(Mascarón de Proa)

La niña de madera no llegó caminando:
allí de pronto estuvo sentada en los ladrillos,
viejas flores del mar cubrían su cabeza,
su mirada tenía tristeza de raíces.

Allí quedó mirando nuestras vidas abiertas,
el ir y ser y andar y volver por la tierra,
el día destiñendo sus pétalos graduales.
Vigilaba sin vernos la niña de madera.

La niña coronada por las antiguas olas,
allí miraba con sus ojos derrotados:
sabía que vivimos en una red remota

de tiempo y agua y olas y sonidos y lluvia,
sin saber si existimos o si somos su sueño.
Ésta es la historia de la muchacha de madera.

(Figurehead of a Ship)

The girl made of wood didn't come here on foot;
suddenly there she was on the beach, sitting on the cobbles,
her head covered with old sea flowers,
her expression the sadness of roots.

There she stayed, watching over our open lives,
the moving and being and going and coming, over the earth,
as the day faded its gradual petals. She watched
over us without seeing us, the girl made of wood:

crowned by ancient waves, she looked out
through her shipwrecked eyes.
She knew we live in a distant net

of time and water and waves and noise and rain,
without knowing if we exist, or if we are her dream.
This is the story of the girl made of wood.

Tal vez no ser es ser sin que tú seas,
sin que vayas cortando el mediodía
como una flor azul, sin que camines
más tarde por la niebla y los ladrillos,

sin esa luz que llevas en la mano
que tal vez otros no verán dorada,
que tal vez nadie supo que crecía
como el origen rojo de la rosa,

sin que seas, en fin, sin que vinieras
brusca, incitante, a conocer mi vida,
ráfaga de rosal, trigo del viento,

y desde entonces soy porque tú eres,
y desde entonces eres, soy y somos,
y por amor seré, serás, seremos.

*M*aybe nothingness is to be without your presence,
without you moving, slicing the noon
like a blue flower, without you walking
later through the fog and the cobbles,

without the light you carry in your hand,
golden, which maybe others will not see,
which maybe no one knew was growing
like the red beginnings of a rose.

In short, without your presence: without your coming
suddenly, incitingly, to know my life,
gust of a rosebush, wheat of wind:

since then I am because you are,
since then you are, I am, we are,
and through love I will be, you will be, we'll be.

*T*al vez herido voy sin ir sangriento
por uno de los rayos de tu vida
y a media selva me detiene el agua:
la lluvia que se cae con su cielo.

Entonces toco el corazón llovido:
allí sé que tus ojos penetraron
por la región extensa de mi duelo
y un susurro de sombra surge solo:

Quién es? Quién es? Pero no tuvo nombre
la hoja o el agua oscura que palpita
a media selva, sorda, en el camino,

y así, amor mío, supe que fui herido
y nadie hablaba allí sino la sombra,
la noche errante, el beso de la lluvia.

Maybe—though I do not bleed—I am wounded, walking
along one of the rays of your life.
In the middle of the jungle the water stops me,
the rain that falls with its sky.

Then I touch the heart that fell, raining:
there I know it was your eyes
that pierced me, into my grief's vast hinterlands.
And only a shadow's whisper appears,

Who is it? Who is it?, but it has no name,
the leaf or dark water that patters
in the middle of the jungle, deaf along the paths:

so, my love, I knew that I was wounded,
and no one spoke there except the shadows,
the wandering night, the kiss of the rain.

De pena en pena cruza sus islas el amor
y establece raíces que luego riega el llanto,
y nadie puede, nadie puede evadir los pasos
del corazón que corre callado y carnicero.

Así tú y yo buscamos un hueco, otro planeta
en donde no tocara la sal tu cabellera,
en donde no crecieran dolores por mi culpa,
en donde viva el pan sin agonía.

Un planeta enredado por distancia y follajes,
un páramo, una piedra cruel y deshabitada,
con nuestras propias manos hacer un nido duro

queríamos, sin daño ni herida ni palabra,
y no fue así el amor, sino una ciudad loca
donde la gente palidece en los balcones.

*L*ove crosses its islands, from grief to grief,
it sets its roots, watered with tears,
and no one—no one—can escape the heart's progress
as it runs, silent and carnivorous.

You and I searched for a wide valley, for another planet
where the salt wouldn't touch your hair,
where sorrows couldn't grow because of anything I did,
where bread could live and not grow old.

A planet entwined with vistas and foliage,
a plain, a rock, hard and unoccupied:
we wanted to build a strong nest

with our own hands, without hurt or harm or speech,
but love was not like that: love was a lunatic city
with crowds of people blanching on their porches.

*A*mor mío, el invierno regresa a sus cuarteles,
establece la tierra sus dones amarillos
y pasamos la mano sobre un país remoto,
sobre la cabellera de la geografía.

Irnos! Hoy! Adelante, ruedas, naves, campanas,
aviones acerados por el diurno infinito
hacia el olor nupcial del archipiélago,
por longitudinales harinas de usufructo!

Vamos, levántate, y endiadémate y sube
y baja y corre y trina con el aire y conmigo
vámonos a los trenes de Arabia o Tocopilla,

sin más que trasmigrar hacia el polen lejano,
a pueblos lancinantes de harapos y gardenias
gobernados por pobres monarcas sin zapatos.

Мy love, winter returns to its billet,
the earth fixes its yellow gifts,
and we caress a distant land,
stroking the hair of the globe—

To leave! now! go: wheels, ships, bells,
airplanes whetted by infinite daylight,
toward the archipelago's nuptial odor,
longitudinal grains of joy!

Let's go—get up—pin back your hair—take off
and land, run and sing with the air and me:
let's take a train to Arabia, or Tocopilla,

only sailing like a distant pollen:
to piercing lands of rags and gardenias,
ruled by indigent monarchs with no shoes.

Recordarás tal vez aquel hombre afilado
que de la oscuridad salió como un cuchillo
y antes de que supiéramos, sabía:
vio el humo y decidió que venía del fuego.

La pálida mujer de cabellera negra
surgió como un pescado del abismo
y entre los dos alzaron en contra del amor
una máquina armada de dientes numerosos.

Hombre y mujer talaron montañas y jardines,
bajaron a los ríos, treparon por los muros,
subieron por los montes su atroz artillería.

El amor supo entonces que se llamaba amor.
Y cuando levanté mis ojos a tu nombre
tu corazón de pronto dispuso mi camino.

*M*aybe you'll remember that razor-faced man
who slipped out from the dark like a blade
and—before we realized—knew what was there:
he saw the smoke and concluded *fire*.

The pallid woman with black hair
rose like a fish from the abyss,
and the two of them built up a contraption,
armed to the teeth, against love.

Man and woman, they felled mountains and gardens,
they went down to the river, they scaled the walls,
they hoisted their atrocious artillery up the hill.

Then love knew it was called *love*.
And when I lifted my eyes to your name,
suddenly your heart showed me my way.

*E*l camino mojado por el agua de agosto
brilla como si fuera cortado en plena luna,
en plena claridad de la manzana,
en mitad de la fruta del otoño.

Neblina, espacio o cielo, la vaga red del día
crece con fríos sueños, sonidos y pescados,
el vapor de las islas combate la comarca,
palpita el mar sobre la luz de Chile.

Todo se reconcentra como el metal, se esconden
las hojas, el invierno enmascara su estirpe
y sólo ciegos somos, sin cesar, solamente.

Solamente sujetos al cauce sigiloso
del movimiento, adiós, del viaje, del camino:
adiós, caen las lágrimas de la naturaleza.

Wet with the waters of August, the road
shines as if cut through the full moon,
the full light of an apple,
through the middle of the autumn's fruit.

Fog, space, or sky, the vague net of the day
swells with cold dreams, noises, fish,
the steam of the islands fights against the land,
the ocean trembles over the light of Chile.

Everything is concentrated like a metal, leaves
hide, winter conceals its lineage,
and we are the only blind ones, endlessly, alone.

Subject only to the silent causeway
of motion, farewell, of departure, of the road:
farewell, the tears of Nature fall.

Esta es la casa, el mar y la bandera.
Errábamos por otros largos muros.
No hallábamos la puerta ni el sonido
desde la ausencia, como desde muertos.

Y al fin la casa abre su silencio,
entramos a pisar el abandono,
las ratas muertas, el adiós vacío,
el agua que lloró en las cañerías.

Lloró, lloró la casa noche y día,
gimió con las arañas, entreabierta,
se desgranó desde sus ojos negros,

y ahora de pronto la volvemos viva,
la poblamos y no nos reconoce:
tiene que florecer, y no se acuerda.

*H*ere are the house, the sea, the flag.
We wander past other long fences.
We couldn't find the gate, nor the sound
of our absence—as if dead.

At last the house opens its silence,
we enter, step over abandoned stuff,
dead rats, empty farewells,
the water that wept in the pipes.

It wept, the house—wept, day and night;
it whimpered with the spiders, ajar,
it fell apart, with its darkened eyes—

and now, abruptly, we return it to life,
we settle in, and it does not recognize us:
it has to bloom and has forgotten how.

Diego Rivera con la paciencia del oso
buscaba la esmeralda del bosque en la pintura
o el bermellón, la flor súbita de la sangre,
recogía la luz del mundo en tu retrato.

Pintaba el imperioso traje de tu nariz,
la centella de tus pupilas desbocadas,
tus uñas que alimentan la envidia de la luna,
y en tu piel estival, tu boca de sandía.

Te puso dos cabezas de volcán encendidas
por fuego, por amor, por estirpe araucana,
y sobre los dos rostros dorados de la greda

te cubrió con el casco de un incendio bravío
y allí secretamente quedaron enredados
mis ojos en su torre total: tu cabellera.

With the patience of a bear, Diego Rivera
hunted through paint for the forest's emerald,
or vermillion, the blood's sudden flower;
in your picture he gathered the light of the world.

He painted the imperious clothing of your nose,
the spark of your cantering eyes,
your nails that fuel the moon's envy,
and, in your summery skin, the melon of your mouth.

He gave you two heads of molten volcanoes,
for fire, for love, for your Araucan lineage,
and over the two golden faces of clay

he covered you with a helmet of noble fire:
there my eyes lingered, in secret,
tangled in your full and towering hair.

Hoy es hoy con el peso de todo el tiempo ido,
con las alas de todo lo que será mañana,
hoy es el Sur del mar, la vieja edad del agua
y la composición de un nuevo día.

A tu boca elevada a la luz o a la luna
se agregaron los pétalos de un día consumido,
y ayer viene trotando por su calle sombría
para que recordemos su rostro que se ha muerto.

Hoy, ayer y mañana se comen caminando,
consumimos un día como una vaca ardiente,
nuestro ganado espera con sus días contados,

pero en tu corazón el tiempo echó su harina,
mi amor construyó un horno con barro de Temuco:
tú eres el pan de cada día para mi alma.

*T*oday is today, with the weight of all past time,
with the wings of all that will be tomorrow;
today is the South of the sea, water's old age,
the composition of a new day.

The petals of a finished day collected on your mouth,
lifted to the light or to the moon,
and yesterday comes trotting down its darkening path
so we can remember that face of yours that died.

Today, yesterday, and tomorrow pass,
swallowed up, consumed in one day like a burning calf;
our cattle wait with their days numbered,

but in your heart time sprinkled its flour,
my love built an oven of Temuco clay:
you are my soul's daily bread.

LXXVIII

*N*o tengo nunca más, no tengo siempre. En la arena
la victoria dejó sus pies perdidos.
Soy un pobre hombre dispuesto a amar a sus semejantes.
No sé quién eres. Te amo. No doy, no vendo espinas.

Alguien sabrá tal vez que no tejí coronas
sangrientas, que combatí la burla,
y que en verdad llené la pleamar de mi alma.
Yo pagué la vileza con palomas.

Yo no tengo jamás porque distinto
fui, soy, seré. Y en nombre
de mi cambiante amor proclamo la pureza.

La muerte es sólo piedra del olvido.
Te amo, beso en tu boca la alegría.
Traigamos leña. Haremos fuego en la montaña.

I have no never-again, I have no always. In the sand
victory abandoned its footprints.
I am a poor man willing to love his fellow men.
I don't know who you are. I love you. I don't give away thorns,
  and I don't sell them.

Maybe someone will know that I didn't weave crowns
to draw blood; that I fought against mockery;
that I did fill the high tide of my soul with the truth.
I repaid vileness with doves.

I have no never, because I was different—
was, am, will be. And in the name
of my ever-changing love I proclaim a purity.

Death is only the stone of oblivion.
I love you, on your lips I kiss happiness itself.
Let's gather firewood. We'll light a fire on the mountain.

Night / *Noche*

LXXIX

*D*e noche, amada, amarra tu corazón al mío
y que ellos en el sueño derroten las tinieblas
como un doble tambor combatiendo en el bosque
contra el espeso muro de las hojas mojadas.

Nocturna travesía, brasa negra del sueño
interceptando el hilo de las uvas terrestres
con la puntualidad de un tren descabellado
que sombra y piedras frías sin cesar arrastrara.

Por eso, amor, amárrame al movimiento puro,
a la tenacidad que en tu pecho golpea
con las alas de un cisne sumergido,

para que a las preguntas estrelladas del cielo
responda nuestro sueño con una sola llave,
con una sola puerta cerrada por la sombra.

$\mathcal{B}$y night, Love, tie your heart to mine, and the two
together in their sleep will defeat the darkness
like a double drum in the forest, pounding
against the thick wall of wet leaves.

Night travel: black flame of sleep
that snips the threads of the earth's grapes,
punctual as a headlong train that would haul
shadows and cold rocks, endlessly.

Because of this, Love, tie me to a purer motion,
to the constancy that beats in your chest
with the wings of a swan underwater,

so that our sleep might answer all the sky's
starry questions with a single key,
with a single door the shadows had closed.

LXXX

De viajes y dolores yo regresé, amor mío,
a tu voz, a tu mano volando en la guitarra,
al fuego que interrumpe con besos el otoño,
a la circulación de la noche en el cielo.

Para todos los hombres pido pan y reinado,
pido tierra para el labrador sin ventura,
que nadie espere tregua de mi sangre o mi canto.
Pero a tu amor no puedo renunciar sin morirme.

Por eso toca el vals de la serena luna,
la barcarola en el agua de la guitarra
hasta que se doblegue mi cabeza soñando:

que todos los desvelos de mi vida tejieron
esta enramada en donde tu mano vive y vuela
custodiando la noche del viajero dormido.

My love, I returned from travel and sorrow
to your voice, to your hand flying on the guitar,
to the fire interrupting the autumn with kisses,
to the night that circles through the sky.

I ask for bread and dominion for all;
for the worker with no future I ask for land.
May no one expect my blood or my song to rest!
But I cannot give up your love, not without dying.

So: play the waltz of the tranquil moon,
the barcarole, on the fluid guitar,
till my head lolls, dreaming:

for all my life's sleeplessness has woven
this shelter in the grove where your hand lives and flies,
watching over the night of the sleeping traveler.

LXXXI

Ya eres mía. Reposa con tu sueño en mi sueño.
Amor, dolor, trabajos, deben dormir ahora.
Gira la noche sobre sus invisibles ruedas
y junto a mí eres pura como el ámbar dormido.

Ninguna más, amor, dormirá con mis sueños.
Irás, iremos juntos por las aguas del tiempo.
Ninguna viajará por la sombra conmigo,
sólo tú, siempreviva, siempre sol, siempre luna.

Ya tus manos abrieron los puños delicados
y dejaron caer suaves signos sin rumbo,
tus ojos se cerraron como dos alas grises,

mientras yo sigo el agua que llevas y me lleva:
la noche, el mundo, el viento devanan su destino,
y ya no soy sin ti sino sólo tu sueño.

172

And now you're mine. Rest with your dream in my dream.
Love and pain and work should all sleep, now.
The night turns on its invisible wheels,
and you are pure beside me as a sleeping amber.

No one else, Love, will sleep in my dreams. You will go,
we will go together, over the waters of time.
No one else will travel through the shadows with me,
only you, evergreen, ever sun, ever moon.

Your hands have already opened their delicate fists
and let their soft drifting signs drop away;
your eyes closed like two gray wings, and I move

after, following the folding water you carry, that carries
me away. The night, the world, the wind spin out their destiny.
Without you, I am your dream, only that, and that is all.

LXXXII

Amor mío, al cerrar esta puerta nocturna
te pido, amor, un viaje por oscuro recinto:
cierra tus sueños, entra con tu cielo en mis ojos,
extiéndete en mi sangre como en un ancho río.

Adiós, adiós, cruel claridad que fue cayendo
en el saco de cada día del pasado,
adiós a cada rayo de reloj o naranja,
salud oh sombra, intermitente compañera!

En esta nave o agua o muerte o nueva vida,
una vez más unidos, dormidos, resurrectos,
somos el matrimonio de la noche en la sangre.

No sé quién vive o muere, quién reposa o despierta,
pero es tu corazón el que reparte
en mi pecho los dones de la aurora.

*A*s we close this nocturnal door, my love,
come with me, through the shadowy places.
Close your dreams, Love, enter my eyes with your skies,
spread out through my blood like a wide river.

Good-bye to the cruel daylight, which dropped
into the gunneysack of the past, each day of it.
Good-bye to every ray of watches or of oranges.
O shadow, my intermittent friend, welcome!

In this ship, or water, or death, or new life,
we are united again, asleep, resurrected:
we are the night's marriage in the blood.

I don't know who it is who lives or dies, who rests or wakes,
but it is your heart that distributes
all the graces of the daybreak, in my breast.

*E*s bueno, amor, sentirte cerca de mí en la noche,
invisible en tu sueño, seriamente nocturna,
mientras yo desenredo mis preocupaciones
como si fueran redes confundidas.

Ausente, por los sueños tu corazón navega,
pero tu cuerpo así abandonado respira
buscándome sin verme, completando mi sueño
como una planta que se duplica en la sombra.

Erguida, serás otra que vivirá mañana,
pero de las fronteras perdidas en la noche,
de este ser y no ser en que nos encontramos

algo queda acercándonos en la luz de la vida
como si el sello de la sombra señalara
con fuego sus secretas criaturas.

It's good to feel you close in the night, Love,
invisible in your sleep, earnestly nocturnal,
while I untangle my confusions
like bewildered nets.

Absent, your heart sails through dreams,
but your body breathes, abandoned like this,
searching for me without seeing me, completing my sleep,
like a plant that propagates in the dark.

When you arise, alive, tomorrow, you'll be someone else:
but something is left from the lost frontiers of the night,
from that being and nothing where we find ourselves,

something that brings us close in the light of life,
as if the seal of the darkness
branded its secret creatures with a fire.

Una vez más, amor, la red del día extingue
trabajos, ruedas, fuegos, estertores, adioses,
y a la noche entregamos el trigo vacilante
que el mediodía obtuvo de la luz y la tierra.

Sólo la luna en medio de su página pura
sostiene las columnas del estuario del cielo,
la habitación adopta la lentitud del oro
y van y van tus manos preparando la noche.

Oh amor, oh noche, oh cúpula cerrada por un río
de impenetrables aguas en la sombra del cielo
que destaca y sumerge sus uvas tempestuosas,

hasta que sólo somos un solo espacio oscuro,
una copa en que cae la ceniza celeste,
una gota en el pulso de un lento y largo río.

Once again, Love, the day's net extinguishes
work, wheels, fires, snores, good-byes,
and we surrender to the night the waving wheat
that noon took from the light and from the earth.

Only the moon, in the center of its white page,
supports the columns of the heaven's harbor,
the bedroom takes on the slowness of gold,
and your hands move, beginning to prepare the night.

O love, O night, O dome surrounded by a river
of impenetrable waters in the shadows of a sky
that lights and sinks its stormy grapes:

till we are only one dark space,
a chalice filling with celestial ashes,
a drop in the pulse of a long slow river.

Del mar hacia las calles corre la vaga niebla
como el vapor de un buey enterrado en el frío,
y largas lenguas de agua se acumulan cubriendo
el mes que a nuestras vidas prometió ser celeste.

Adelantado otoño, panal silbante de hojas,
cuando sobre los pueblos palpita tu estandarte
cantan mujeres locas despidiendo a los ríos,
los caballos relinchan hacia la Patagonia.

Hay una enredadera vespertina en tu rostro
que crece silenciosa por el amor llevada
hasta las herraduras crepitantes del cielo.

Me inclino sobre el fuego de tu cuerpo nocturno
y no sólo tus senos amo sino el otoño
que esparce por la niebla su sangre ultramarina.

The vague fog flows from the sea toward the streets
like the steam-breath of cattle buried in the cold,
and long tongues of water gather, covering the month
that our lives had been promised would be heavenly.

Autumn on the march, whistling honeycomb of leaves,
when your standards fly over our towns
crazy women sing good-bye to the rivers,
horses whinny toward Patagonia.

On your face is an evening vine,
climbing silently, that love lifts
up toward the crackling horseshoes of the sky.

I bend toward the fire of your nocturnal body, and I love
not only your breasts but autumn, too, as it spreads
its ultramarine blood through the fog.

LXXXVI

Oh Cruz del Sur, oh trébol de fósforo fragante,
con cuatro besos hoy penetró tu hermosura
y atravesó la sombra y mi sombrero:
la luna iba redonda por el frío.

Entonces con mi amor, con mi amada, oh diamantes
de escarcha azul, serenidad del cielo,
espejo, apareciste y se llenó la noche
con tus cuatro bodegas temblorosas de vino.

Oh palpitante plata de pez pulido y puro,
cruz verde, perejil de la sombra radiante,
luciérnaga a la unidad del cielo condenada,

descansa en mí, cerremos tus ojos y los míos.
Por un minuto duerme con la noche del hombre.
Enciende en mí tus cuatro números constelados.

O Southern Cross, O clover of fragrant phosphorous:
it entered your body today with four holy kisses,
it traveled across the shadows and across my hat,
and the moon went circling through the cold.

Then—with my love, with my dearest—diamonds
of blue frost, calm of the sky, mirror:
you appeared, and the night filled
with your four trembling cellars of wine.

O throbbing silver of a pure polished fish,
green cross, parsley of the radiant shadows,
firefly condemned to the wholeness of the sky:

rest on me, let us close your eyes, and mine.
For one moment, sleep with the human night.
Light your four-sided constellation in me.

LXXXVII

*L*as tres aves del mar, tres rayos, tres tijeras,
cruzaron por el cielo frío hacia Antofagasta,
por eso quedó el aire tembloroso,
todo tembló como bandera herida.

Soledad, dame el signo de tu incesante origen,
el apenas camino de los pájaros crueles,
y la palpitación que sin duda precede
a la miel, a la música, al mar, al nacimiento.

(Soledad sostenida por un constante rostro
como una grave flor sin cesar extendida
hasta abarcar la pura muchedumbre del cielo.)

Volaban alas frías del mar, del Archipiélago,
hacia la arena del Noroeste de Chile.
Y la noche cerró su celeste cerrojo.

*T*hree birds of the sea, three sunbeams, three scissors
crossed the cold sky toward Antofagasta:
that's why the air was left trembling,
why everything trembled like a wounded flag.

Loneliness, give me the sign of your ceaseless origins,
the path—hardly a path—of the cruel birds,
the palpitation that surely comes
before honey, music, the sea, a birth.

(Loneliness sustained by a constant face—
like a calm slow flower, constantly held out—
till it reaches the pure swarming throngs of the sky.)

Cold wings of the sea, of the archipelago, went
flying toward the sands of northeast Chile.
The night slid shut its heavenly bolt.

El mes de marzo vuelve con su luz escondida
y se deslizan peces inmensos por el cielo,
vago vapor terrestre progresa sigiloso,
una por una caen al silencio las cosas.

Por suerte en esta crisis de atmósfera errabunda
reuniste las vidas del mar con las del fuego,
el movimiento gris de la nave de invierno,
la forma que el amor imprimió a la guitarra.

Oh amor, rosa mojada por sirenas y espumas,
fuego que baila y sube la invisible escalera
y despierta en el túnel del insomnio a la sangre

para que se consuman las olas en el cielo,
olvide el mar sus bienes y leones
y caiga el mundo adentro de las redes oscuras.

March returns with its secretive light,
immense fish glide through the sky,
vague terrestrial vapors move along quietly,
one by one all things succumb to the silence.

In this crisis of the wandering weather, luckily
you joined the sea's lives to the fire's lives:
gray motions of the ship of winter,
the shape that love impressed on the guitar.

O love, O rose moistened by the mermaids and the foam,
fire that dances and climbs invisible stairs,
that wakes the blood in the tunnels of sleeplessness:

so that the waves may exhaust themselves in the sky,
the sea forget its goods and its lions,
the world drop into the shadowy nets.

Cuando yo muero quiero tus manos en mis ojos:
quiero la luz y el trigo de tus manos amadas
pasar una vez más sobre mí su frescura:
sentir la suavidad que cambió mi destino.

Quiero que vivas mientras yo, dormido, te espero,
quiero que tus oídos sigan oyendo el viento,
que huelas el aroma del mar que amamos juntos
y que sigas pisando la arena que pisamos.

Quiero que lo que amo siga vivo
y a ti te amé y canté sobre todas las cosas,
por eso sigue tú floreciendo, florida,

para que alcances todo lo que mi amor te ordena,
para que se pasee mi sombra por tu pelo,
para que así conozcan la razón de mi canto.

*W*hen I die, I want your hands on my eyes:
I want the light and wheat of your beloved hands
to pass their freshness over me once more:
I want to feel the softness that changed my destiny.

I want you to live while I wait for you, asleep.
I want your ears still to hear the wind, I want you
to sniff the sea's aroma that we loved together,
to continue to walk on the sand we walk on.

I want what I love to continue to live,
and you whom I love and sang above everything else
to continue to flourish, full-flowered:

so that you can reach everything my love directs you to,
so that my shadow can travel along in your hair,
so that everything can learn the reason for my song.

Pensé morir, sentí de cerca el frío,
y de cuanto viví sólo a ti te dejaba:
tu boca eran mi día y mi noche terrestres
y tu piel la república fundada por mis besos.

En ese instante se terminaron los libros,
la amistad, los tesoros sin tregua acumulados,
la casa transparente que tú y yo construimos:
todo dejó de ser, menos tus ojos.

Porque el amor, mientras la vida nos acosa,
es simplemente una ola alta sobre las olas,
pero ay cuando la muerte viene a tocar la puerta

hay sólo tu mirada para tanto vacío,
sólo tu claridad para no seguir siendo,
sólo tu amor para cerrar la sombra.

I thought I was dying, I felt the cold up close
and knew that from all my life I left only you behind:
my earthly day and night were your mouth,
your skin the republic my kisses founded.

In that instant the books stopped,
and friendship, treasures restlessly amassed,
the transparent house that you and I built:
everything dropped away, except your eyes.

Because while life harasses us, love is
only a wave taller than the other waves:
but oh, when death comes knocking at the gate,

there is only your glance against so much emptiness,
only your light against extinction,
only your love to shut out the shadows.

La edad nos cubre como la llovizna,
interminable y árido es el tiempo,
una pluma de sal toca tu rostro,
una gotera carcomió mi traje:

el tiempo no distingue entre mis manos
o un vuelo de naranjas en las tuyas:
pica con nieve y azadón la vida:
la vida tuya que es la vida mía.

La vida mía que te di se llena
de años, como el volumen de un racimo.
Regresarán las uvas a la tierra.

Y aún allá abajo el tiempo sigue siendo,
esperando, lloviendo sobre el polvo,
ávido de borrar hasta la ausencia.

Age covers us like drizzle;
time is interminable and sad;
a salt feather touches your face;
a trickle ate through my shirt.

Time does not distinguish between my hands
and a flock of oranges in yours:
with snow and picks life chips away
at your life, which is my life.

My life, which I gave you, fills
with years like a swelling cluster of fruit.
The grapes will return to the earth.

And even down there time
continues, waiting, raining
on the dust, eager to erase even absence.

Amor mío, si muero y tú no mueres,
amor mío, si mueres y no muero,
no demos al dolor más territorio:
no hay extensión como la que vivimos.

Polvo en el trigo, arena en las arenas
el tiempo, el agua errante, el viento vago
nos llevó como grano navegante.
Pudimos no encontrarnos en el tiempo.

Esta pradera en que nos encontramos,
oh pequeño infinito! devolvemos.
Pero este amor, amor, no ha terminado,

y así como no tuvo nacimiento
no tiene muerte, es como un largo río,
sólo cambia de tierras y de labios.

My love, if I die and you don't—,
My love, if you die and I don't—,
let's not give grief an even greater field.
No expanse is greater than where we live.

Dust in the wheat, sand in the deserts,
time, wandering water, the vague wind
swept us on like sailing seeds.
We might not have found one another in time.

This meadow where we find ourselves,
O little infinity! we give it back.
But Love, this love has not ended:

just as it never had a birth, it has
no death: it is like a long river,
only changing lands, and changing lips.

Si alguna vez tu pecho se detiene,
si algo deja de andar ardiendo por tus venas,
si tu voz en tu boca se va sin ser palabra,
si tus manos se olvidan de volar y se duermen,

Matilde, amor, deja tus labios entreabiertos
porque ese último beso debe durar conmigo,
debe quedar inmóvil para siempre en tu boca
para que así también me acompañe en mi muerte.

Me moriré besando tu loca boca fría,
abrazando el racimo perdido de tu cuerpo,
y buscando la luz de tus ojos cerrados.

Y así cuando la tierra reciba nuestro abrazo
iremos confundidos en una sola muerte
a vivir para siempre la eternidad de un beso.

If some time your breast pauses, if something stops
moving, stops burning through your veins,
if the voice in your mouth escapes without becoming word,
if your hands forget to fly, and fall asleep,

Matilde, my love, leave your lips half-open:
because that final kiss should linger with me,
it should stay still, forever, in your mouth,
so that it goes with me, too, into my death.

I will die kissing your crazy cold mouth,
caressing the lost fruit buds of your body,
looking for the light of your closed eyes.

And so when the earth receives our embrace
we will go blended in a single death, forever
living the eternity of a kiss.

Si muero sobrevíveme con tanta fuerza pura
que despiertes la furia del pálido y del frío,
de sur a sur levanta tus ojos indelebles,
de sol a sol que suene tu boca de guitarra.

No quiero que vacilen tu risa ni tus pasos,
no quiero que se muera mi herencia de alegría,
no llames a mi pecho, estoy ausente.
Vive en mi ausencia como en una casa.

Es una casa tan grande la ausencia
que pasarás en ella a través de los muros
y colgarás los cuadros en el aire.

Es una casa tan transparente la ausencia
que yo sin vida te veré vivir
y si sufres, mi amor, me moriré otra vez.

If I die, survive me with such a pure force
you make the pallor and the coldness rage;
flash your indelible eyes from south to south,
from sun to sun, till your mouth sings like a guitar.

I don't want your laugh or your footsteps to waver;
I don't want my legacy of happiness to die;
don't call to my breast: I'm not there.
Live in my absence as in a house.

Absence is such a large house
that you'll walk through the walls,
hang pictures in sheer air.

Absence is such a transparent house
that even being dead I will see you there,
and if you suffer, Love, I'll die a second time.

Quiénes se amaron como nosotros? Busquemos
las antiguas cenizas del corazón quemado
y allí que caigan uno por uno nuestros besos
hasta que resucite la flor deshabitada.

Amemos el amor que consumió su fruto
y descendió a la tierra con rostro y poderío:
tú y yo somos la luz que continúa,
su inquebrantable espiga delicada.

Al amor sepultado por tanto tiempo frío,
por nieve y primavera, por olvido y otoño,
acerquemos la luz de una nueva manzana,

de la frescura abierta por una nueva herida,
como el amor antiguo que camina en silencio
por una eternidad de bocas enterradas.

*W*hoever loved as we did? Let us hunt
for the ancient cinders of a heart that burned
and make our kisses fall one by one,
till that empty flower rises again.

Let us love the love that consumed its fruit and went
down, its image and its power, into the earth:
you and I are the light that endures,
its irrevocable delicate thorn.

Bring to that love, entombed by so much cold time,
by snow and spring, by oblivion and autumn,
the light of a new apple, light

of a freshness opened by a new wound,
like that ancient love that passes in silence
through an eternity of buried mouths.

*P*ienso, esta época en que tú me amaste
se irá por otra azul substituida,
será otra piel sobre los mismos huesos,
otros ojos verán la primavera.

Nadie de los que ataron esta hora,
de los que conversaron con el humo,
gobiernos, traficantes, transeúntes,
continuarán moviéndose en sus hilos.

Se irán los crueles dioses con anteojos,
los peludos carnívoros con libro,
los pulgones y los pipipasseyros.

Y cuando esté recién lavado el mundo
nacerán otros ojos en el agua
y crecerá sin lágrimas el trigo.

I think this time when you loved me
will pass away, and another blue will replace it;
another skin will cover the same bones;
other eyes will see the spring.

None of those who tried to tie time down—
those who dealt in smoke,
bureaucrats, businessmen, transients—none
will keep moving, tangled in their ropes.

The cruel gods wearing spectacles will pass away,
the hairy carnivore with the book,
the little green fleas and the pitpit birds.

And when the earth is freshly washed,
other eyes will be born in the water,
the wheat will flourish without tears.

*H*ay que volar en este tiempo, a dónde?
Sin alas, sin avión, volar sin duda:
ya los pasos pasaron sin remedio,
no elevaron los pies del pasajero.

Hay que volar a cada instante como
las águilas, las moscas y los días,
hay que vencer los ojos de Saturno
y establecer allí nuevas campanas.

Ya no bastan zapatos ni caminos,
ya no sirve la tierra a los errantes,
ya cruzaron la noche las raíces,

y tú aparecerás en otra estrella
determinadamente transitoria
convertida por fin en amapola.

These days, one must fly—but where to?
without wings, without an airplane, fly—without a doubt:
the footsteps have passed on, to no avail;
they didn't move the feet of the traveler along.

At every instant, one must fly—like
eagles, like houseflies, like days:
must conquer the rings of Saturn
and build new carillons there.

Shoes and pathways are no longer enough,
the earth is no use anymore to the wanderer:
the roots have already crossed through the night,

and you will appear on another planet,
stubbornly transient,
transformed in the end into poppies.

Y esta palabra, este papel escrito
por las mil manos de una sola mano,
no queda en ti, no sirve para sueños,
cae a la tierra: allí se continúa.

No importa que la luz o la alabanza
se derramen y salgan de la copa
si fueron un tenaz temblor del vino,
si se tiñó tu boca de amaranto.

No quiere más la sílaba tardía,
lo que trae y retrae el arrecife
de mis recuerdos, la irritada espuma,

no quiere más sino escribir tu nombre.
Y aunque lo calle mi sombrío amor
más tarde lo dirá la primavera.

*A*nd this word, this paper the thousand hands
of a single hand have written on, does not remain
inside you, it is no good for dreaming.
It falls to the earth; there it continues.

No matter that the light, or praise,
spilled over the rim of the cup,
if they were a willful shimmer in the wine,
if your mouth were stained purple as amaranth.

This word: it no longer wants the slow-spoken syllable,
what the reef brings, and brings back,
from my memories, the churned foam:

it wants nothing but to write your name.
And even though my brooding love silences it
now, later the springtime will pronounce it.

*O*tros días vendrán, será entendido
el silencio de plantas y planetas
y cuántas cosas puras pasarán!
Tendrán olor a luna los violines!

El pan será tal vez como tú eres:
tendrá tu voz, tu condición de trigo,
y hablarán otras cosas con tu voz:
los caballos perdidos del otoño.

Aunque no sea como está dispuesto
el amor llenará grandes barricas
como la antigua miel de los pastores,

y tú en el polvo de mi corazón
(en donde habrán inmensos almacenes)
irás y volverás entre sandías.

Other days will come, the silence
of plants and of planets will be understood,
and so many pure things will happen!
Violins will have the fragrance of the moon!

Maybe the bread will be like you:
it will have your voice, your wheat,
and other things—the lost horses
of autumn—will speak with your voice.

And even if it's not what you'd prefer, exactly,
love will fill huge barrels
like the ancient honey of the shepherds,

and there in the dust of my heart (where
so many plentiful things will be stored),
you will come and go among the melons.

$\mathcal{E}$n medio de la tierra apartaré
las esmeraldas para divisarte
y tú estarás copiando las espigas
con una pluma de agua mensajera.

Qué mundo! Qué profundo perejil!
Qué nave navegando en la dulzura!
Y tú tal vez y yo tal vez topacio!
Ya no habrá división en las campanas.

Ya no habrá sino todo el aire libre,
las manzanas llevadas por el viento,
el suculento libro en la enramada,

y allí donde respiran los claveles
fundaremos un traje que resista
la eternidad de un beso victorioso.

In the center of the earth I will push aside
the emeralds so that I can see you—
you like an amanuensis, with a pen
of water, copying the green sprigs of plants.

What a world! What deep parsley!
What a ship sailing through the sweetness!
And you, maybe—and me, maybe—a topaz.
There'll be no more dissensions in the bells.

There won't be anything but all the fresh air,
apples carried on the wind,
the succulent book in the woods:

and there where the carnations breathe, we will begin
to make ourselves a clothing, something to last
through the eternity of a victorious kiss.

NOTES

Dedica-
tion
Matilde: Pablo Neruda began to live with Matilde Urrutia, later his third wife, in 1955. During 1955–1957, while he was writing the *One Hundred Love Sonnets*, Neruda was working also on the *Elemental Odes*, on *Extravagaria*, and on *The Captain's Verses*, addressed to Matilde. (He withheld the latter collection from publication for some time, out of delicacy for the feelings of Delia del Carril, his wife of eighteen years, from whom he had separated in September 1955.) *One Hundred Love Sonnets* was published in 1960. He was awarded the Nobel Prize in Literature in 1971; he died in 1973, during the week of the coup that overthrew Salvador Allende's Popular Unity government. Matilde Neruda died in January 1985.

II, 4
Taltal: A small seaport town outside the city of Antofagasta, in the bleak nitrate highlands of north-central Chile (see note to LXXXVII, 2).

10
Boroa: An adjective made from "Boro," the name of a pre-Incan Indian tribe, their language, and their territory, which includes parts of modern Peru, Brazil, and Colombia. The Boro lies essentially in a large ring around Iquitos, Peru, in the rocky, lush, and water-webbed headlands of the Amazon River, where it conjoins dozens of smaller rivers.

V, 5
Quinchimalí: A small town outside Chillán, south of Santiago, famous—like Chillán—for its clay soil and for its rare "black" pottery (see note to XV, 8).

6
Frontera: The volcanic, snow-capped wilderness-frontier along the coast near where Neruda spent his childhood is generically called the Frontera.

9
Arauca: Neruda grew up in the rugged rainy frontier territory south of Concepción, near the town of Temuco, on

the Pacific littoral in the south of Chile; Matilde Urrutia was born in Chillán, also in the South, one hundred miles from Temuco (see note to XV, 8). The town of Temuco was founded only late in the nineteenth century, by Araucanian Indians, under treaty with the Chilean central administration. For centuries the independent Araucanians had resisted harsh and sometimes vicious campaigns by the Incas, the Spanish, and the Chilean government, itself, to conquer or to colonize them. In "Macchu Picchu" and other poems Neruda makes them (and the region, "Araucania" or "Arauca") a metaphor of the political autonomy and integrity of Chile—and sometimes of South America as a whole.

XI, 14   *Quitratúe*: In 1875 the population of the Quetratúe (or Quitratúe) people—a subtribe of the Araucanians—was 160. Now the name applies primarily to the small region of the desolate volcanic and glacial highlands of Arauca, just south of Temuco, which was once theirs—including Lake Panguipulli (literally, "puma hill").

XV, 8   *Chillán*: Matilde Urrutia's birthplace, a dramatically mountainous region (and volcano) south of Santiago. An earthquake devastated Chillán in 1939; Neruda was partly responsible for the famous murals there by David Alfaro Siqueiros, painted during the rebuilding of the city.

XIX, 1   *Isla Negra*: From 1939 on, Neruda spent much of his time on Isla Negra, in central Chile, in his house overlooking the sea. In 1955 he and Matilde moved into a house he had built there, La Chascona. In 1959 they built La Sebastiana, in Valparaíso.

XXII, 6   *Angol*: The capital city of the province of Malleco, in Arauco, just south of Chillán.

XXVI, 1   *Iquique*: Fishing and tourist city in the north of Chile, with magnificent white sand beaches, some of them miles long.

2   *Río Dulce*: River in Guatemala with open harbors at its mouth (literally, "Sweet River").

XXX, 1   *Archipelago*: South of Temuco the rest of Chile is primarily an archipelago—or, more properly, a series of archipelagoes—of thousands of wild islands.

XXXI, 2   *Lota*: A territory and a city fifty miles from Chillán, on the Pacific, in the province of Concepción, famous for its herbal lushness and its coal mines.

XXXIII, 2   In 1955–56 the Nerudas traveled to the Soviet Union, China, and several other socialist countries, as well as to France and Italy. On their return to America he read in Brazil and Uruguay, and they spent several months in Totoral, Córdoba, Argentina.

XLI, 1   *January*: In the Southern Hemisphere, January is the height of the hot season, mid-summer; see also, for instance, LXXIV, 1, for August as late winter/early spring and LXXXVIII, 1, for March as autumn.

L, 1   *Cotapos*: Acario Cotapos, the Chilean composer famous also for his stories and anecdotes, was a friend of Neruda in Santiago.

LVII, 1   *Liars*: In the 1950s Neruda came under attack in some literary circles for abandoning the surrealist lyricism of his early work and for writing more politically declarative populist poems.

LIX   *G. M.*: Apparently, Gabriela Mistral (Lucila Godoy Alcayaga). Mistral, who was awarded the 1945 Nobel Prize in Literature, had been the headmistress of the local school in Temuco while Neruda was growing up there. Though they did not know one another then, later they were friends. Mistral died in January 1957, while Neruda was working on these poems. (See also note to LXVII.)

LXVIII   *Figurehead*: Neruda avidly collected the figureheads of old sailing ships. One, the María Celeste, which he kept on the beach outside his house, was said to weep real tears each winter. Another, which Neruda claimed resembled Gabriela Mistral, so intrigued pious local women that the Nerudas had to discourage them from kneeling to it and offering it lighted candles and flowers, as to a cult figure.

LXXII, 11   *Tocopilla*: A seaport in the stark northern province of Antofagasta (see note to LXXXVII, 2), center of nitrate processing and of copper mining from the Chuquicamata mines.

LXXVI, 1   *Diego Rivera*: While serving as Chile's consul general in Mexico from 1940 to 1943, Neruda got to know the Mexican painter Diego Rivera and to admire his socialist, populist murals.

LXXVII, 13   *Temuca*: See note to V, 6 and 9.

LXXXV, 8   *Patagonia*: The semi-arid, wind-ripped plateau at the southernmost end of the South American continent.

LXXXVI, 1   *Southern Cross*: The high four-lobed constellation is a sign of winter in the Southern Hemisphere.

LXXVII, 2   *Antofagasta*: This mountainous desert province in north-central Chile has the highest solar intensity of any place in the world. Birds flying toward Antofagasta (and beyond, line 13) are flying north for the winter.

INDEX OF FIRST LINES

You sing, and your voice peels the husk   *111*
You will remember that leaping stream   *13*

Acostúmbrate a ver detrás de mí la sombra   *120*
Al golpe de la ola contra la piedra indócil   *22*
Amo el trozo de tierra que tú eres   *36*
Amor, ahora nos vamos a la casa   *72*
Amor, amor, las nubes a la torre del cielo   *52*
Amor, cuántos caminos hasta llegar a un beso,   *8*
Amor, de grano a grano, de planeta a planeta,   *60*
Amor mío, al cerrar esta puerta nocturna   *174*
Amor mío, el invierno regresa a sus cuarteles,   *152*
Amor mío, si muero y tú no mueres,   *194*
Antes de amarte, amor, nada era mío: *54*
Aquí está el pan, el vino, la mesa, la morada: *112*
Áspero amor, violeta coronada de espinas,   *10*
A ti te hiere aquel que quiso hacerme daño,   *128*
Ay de mí, ay de nosotros, bienamada,   *132*
Cantas, y a sol y a cielo con tu canto   *110*
Con laureles del Sur y orégano de Lota   *66*
Corazón mío, reina del apio y de la artesa: *78*
Cotapos dice que tu risa cae   *106*
Cuando yo muero quiero tus manos en mis ojos: *188*
Cuántas veces, amor, te amé sin verte y tal vez sin recuerdo,   *48*
De las estrellas que admiré, mojadas   *98*
Del mar hacia las calles corre la vaga niebla   *180*
De noche, amada, amarra tu corazón al mío   *168*
De pena en pena cruza sus islas el amor   *150*
Desde hace mucho tiempo la tierra te conoce: *34*
Desdichas del mes de enero cuando el indiferente   *88*
Desnuda eres tan simple como una de tus manos,   *58*
De tanto amor mi vida se tiñó de violeta   *136*
Detrás de mí en la rama quiero verte.   *100*
De viajes y dolores yo regresé, amor mío,   *170*